Pour Sandie Wiesenthal,

La gourmandise, plaisir indispensable

à la vie ....

A très bientôt au Plaza Paris.

François Perret

FRENCH PASTRY

AT THE RITZ PARIS

FRENCH PASTRY

AT THE RITZ PARIS

FRANÇOIS PERRET

Pastry Chef

Foreword
MICHEL TROISGROS

Photography
BERNHARD WINKELMANN

ABRAMS I NEW YORK

Foreword

A meringue, a dessert, a sponge cake... when it is made by François, it is the smell that first tantalizes your nose, something that is rare in patisserie. But there is also a freshness, like a breath of cool air, that captivates you. And there is the color, the attraction of the cream, either as an ingredient in a cake or as an accompaniment to it. What strikes you immediately about the anthology of his desserts is their elegance and their abundance. They are "enormous": of a size that we are not used to seeing. They stimulate the appetite and call for sharing, which is primordial and something that adds to the pleasure. Already, at 28 years old, when he joined me at the Lancaster to take up his first position as a chef, he exuded this abundance. He is also a peerless technician. Pastry chefs have their own way of doing things that we Chefs know nothing about. It's not that cooking is more empirical, but it seeks less to peel back the layers. With patisserie, finding *the* technical solution is one approach. For that reason, we are complementary. Pastry chefs have enabled cooking to evolve into a Master's degree in astonishing ways. "If you want to cook well, learn patisserie first," said Michel Guérard, the cook who brought to patisserie the freedom to extricate himself from this obsession with technique, letting his sensibility and his emotions express themselves. I have known

by

MICHEL TROISGROS

pastry chefs who do not taste what they have made, their only goal being visual impact. In this regard, I think that my meeting with François was a turning point. It allowed him to take charge of this gustatory and emotional quest and to become the pastry chef he is today. For example, his madeleine has an unbelievable lightness and subtlety. It is a cloud to which honey brings a bitterness that astonishes you, something so rare and so difficult to "control," but—oh—how welcome it is here. It has a voluptuousness that is perfectly balanced. To the delight of our taste buds, François is part of this new generation who have revolutionized sugar. With him, you are miles away from the heavy crème pâtissière and butter creams, which saturate and tire the palate. With each mouthful you want to have a little bit more, and to come back. You are blown away. It is the way of all true creators to capture the world around them and leave their mark on it. His desserts tell stories that are sincere and reveal what inspired them. The smell of a tart drifting through his mother's kitchen, the sight of a picture, a piece of music he remembers... it doesn't matter, directly or indirectly, these little snatches of his past life that he has rediscovered are under our eyes. And they transport us, just like his *barquette* (little caramel boat)—an atomic bomb of flavor!—into his imagination.

CONTENTS

Foreword
MICHEL TROISGROS
5

FRANÇOIS PERRET
by Marie-Catherine de la Roche
8

FIRST PLEASURES OF THE DAY
16

IN THE COURSE OF A LUNCH
38

AFTERNOON TEA REGAINED
64

GRAND EVENING DESSERTS
98

FEASTS GREAT AND SMALL
AROUND THE CLOCK
134

MY PERSONAL FAVORITE
190

E verything inspires him, everything enchants him: the center of a flower, a beautifully carved handle on a door, a piece of honeycomb... "A dessert must arouse desire, its deliciousness must make you want to come back for more," he says with a smile that is half innocent and half that of a cupid ready to make you succumb to the sin of pure indulgence.

The story of François Perret and patisserie is one of exuberance and delight. A delight that evokes the first emotions he felt at big family dining tables where, when it was time for dessert, all conversation was suspended. It was a moment that was fascinating to the darting eyes of an eager child when suddenly the brouhaha of the meal gave way to a silence of blissful contentment. Bewitched by what he saw, he wanted to become an apprentice and, at 16, he took his first step when he began his training, joining a small patisserie in his native town of Bourg-en-Bresse. But, very quickly, his talent began to gather momentum, and he left for Paris and the road to stardom. From Le Meurice, by way of the George V, Hotel Lancaster, and Shangri-La, this road led him to the Ritz Paris. In June 2016, the hotel reopened its doors and opened them to him. The adolescent had reached his Holy Grail and, at 35, here he was in his dream location.

FRANÇOIS PERRET

by Marie-Catherine de la Roche

Since then, this "Pastry Chef of the Year 2017" has recreated a *Tendre* (sweet) menu alongside the menu of chef Nicolas Sale. One wearing a sweet chef's hat, the other a savory chef's hat, these two symbiotic friends formed a harmonious partnership, the strength of which the Michelin Guide immediately recognized, awarding two stars to La Table de L'Espadon and one to its Jardins. It must be said that the desserts of François and the cooking of Nicolas are perfectly complementary, echoing each other with a surprising creativity. And with good reason, as François Perret is not just a baker who allows himself to get stuck in a rut: this pastry chef is also a cook. His creations have a vibrancy, a finesse, and a lightness like no other. Haute couture work that uses "just the right amount of sugar," defines his style. He uses it sparingly, like a seasoning, in small amounts and in an incredibly delicate way, to enhance a dish but never saturate the palate. He doesn't hesitate to juggle with acidity or bitterness to find the moment when flavors combine perfectly to tease the taste buds and unlock pleasure, such as the unexpected delights of a sweet-savory combination or the pairing of a fruit and vegetable in Les Jardins de L'Espadon. Entremets in the Bar Vendôme are reinterpretations that are full of surprises, playful transformations of the great classics, and a madeleine with an ingenuous heart. Or, transmuted

CESAR RITZ
1850 - 1918

A place for a time,
a time for a place.

as a nanoparticle of tenderness in a cloud of milk for "*thé à la française*" (French afternoon tea) in the Salon Proust, a place full of every delight where mischievous dandy biscuit accomplices sit side by side. The happiness of a *pain perdu* rediscovered miraculously on the breakfast table or a favorite family cake that, in a single stroke, transports you back to your childhood. A three-step waltz in a sequence of desserts at La Table de L'Espadon allows time for detours... Whether a simple cake or L'Espadon's triple somersault, everything becomes irresistible. The eyes widen, the mouth enjoys it, asks for more, and the appetite wises up. Because to this demiurge of perpetually restless imagination, abundance is matched only by the taste of truth. In French, we use OVNI to describe both an identified and an unidentified flying object and we can use the same initials to describe François's iconic desserts but, in this case, the initials mean *Objet de Volupté Nommément Identifié* (Voluptuous Identified Object).

Called simply "Rhubarb," "Honey," "Vanilla," the names of these desserts reveal the gentle, passionate emancipation of a patisserie free of all constraints that goes straight to what is fundamental. When it comes to taste, he has a true vocation. Fruits, chocolate nibs, honey... the ingredient is king and he is crazy about it. His art is an uncompromising expression of the celebration of pleasure. And from the valuable hours he has spent on his creations, which have sprung from his inventiveness or by being enchanted once more by his youthful memories, the Ritz Paris offers pure indulgence. An indulgence, he says, that put a sparkle into the eyes of a child ready to play a trick of his own: "start by looking, it will put stars in your eyes, and leave a smile on your lips." In this superb collection of recipes, photographed by Bernhard Winkelmann, from the first brioche of the day to the crumb bouncing back as part of a grand evening dessert at the highest gastronomic level of patisserie, François Perret reveals to us "secrets as big as the Ritz."

The eyes widen, the mouth enjoys it, asks for more, and the appetite wises up.

15

FIRST
PLEASURES
OF THE DAY

SERVES 8
Prep: 20 min.
Cook: about 20 min.

· *1 brioche*
· *2 tbsp. (28 ml) whole milk*
· *1 vanilla bean*
· *¾ cup (6 oz./180 g) egg yolk (about 6 medium yolks)*
· *Scant ⅔ cup (4 oz./115 g) superfine sugar*
· *Scant 3½ cups (800 ml) whipping cream from Étrez, 33% butterfat*
· *Butter and brown sugar, for cooking*

You can make the brioche yourself (see page 28) or buy one from your baker.

In a saucepan, bring the milk and vanilla to a simmer. Remove from the heat, cover and let infuse.

Meanwhile, in a mixing bowl, whisk the egg yolks and sugar together until pale and thickened (the ribbon stage). Add the cream and the infused milk, a little at a time, whisking continuously. Remove the vanilla.

Preheat the oven to 350°F (180°C/Gas mark 4).

Cut the brioche into thick slices and then dip one slice in the cream mixture, making sure it is well soaked. Drain well, letting the excess mixture drip back into the bowl. Repeat with the remaining brioche slices.

Melt a little butter in a skillet and sprinkle over brown sugar. Let caramelize, then add the soaked brioche slices.

Fry the slices until they are caramelized on both sides and then finish cooking in the oven for 1 minute.

Return the slices to the skillet and serve on hot plates.

Brioche French toast

Once the brioche slices have been soaked in the cream mixture, pass the leftover mixture through a fine-mesh sieve and use it to make crèmes brûlées.

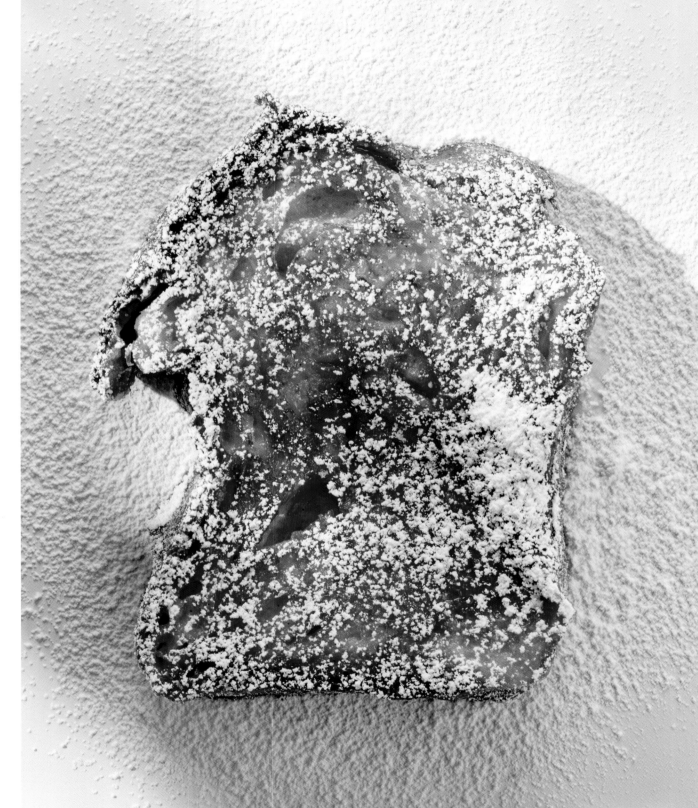

SERVES 10

Prep: 10 min.
Chill: at least 1 hr. or overnight

· 1¾ cups (400 ml)
  whole milk
· ⅓ cup (75 ml) whipping cream
  from Étrez, 33% butterfat
· 4 oz. (110 g) plain yogurt
· 2 tbsp. (1 oz./30 g) brown sugar
· ⅓ tsp. (1 g) finely-grated lemon zest
· 2 tbsp. (30 ml) lemon juice
· Generous 1½ cups (4½ oz./130 g)
  rolled oats
· 1 oz. (30 g) raisins

TO SERVE

· 1 Granny Smith apple
· Juice of 1 lemon
· A mixture of red fruit of
  your choice (strawberries,
  raspberries, blueberries...)

Fresh fruit muesli

The dairy co-operative at Étrez, in the department of Ain, makes high quality AOP (Appellation d'Origine Protégée) products that I use regularly in my recipes, in particular cream and butter from Bresse.

In a cold bowl, mix together the milk, cream, yogurt, brown sugar, lemon zest, and lemon juice. Add the oats and raisins and chill for at least 1 hour or overnight.

The next day, just before serving, cut the apple into julienne strips and immerse them in a small bowl of water with the lemon juice added to prevent the apple discoloring. Drain and carefully pat dry with paper towel.

Serve the muesli topped with the apple julienne and red fruit.

Waffles

SERVES 5–6

Prep: 10 min.
Cook: time depends on your waffle maker

- *1½ cups (12 oz./340 g) egg white (about 12 medium whites)*
- *1½ tsp. (7.5 g) fine-grain salt*
- *⅓ cup (2 oz./55 g) brown sugar*
- *Scant 1 cup (6¾ oz./190 g) butter from Étrez*
- *½ tsp. (2.5 g) ground vanilla bean powder*
- *1½ cups (350 ml) whole milk*
- *2½ cups (11 oz./310 g) all-purpose flour*

TO SERVE

- *Confectioners' sugar, Chantilly cream (see page 40), and grated chocolate*

Put the egg whites, salt, and brown sugar in the bowl of a stand mixer fitted with the whisk attachment and whisk until they form peaks.

In a saucepan, bring the butter and vanilla powder to a boil. Add the cold milk and strain through a fine-mesh sieve.

Sift the flour into another bowl and, using an electric hand mixer, whisk on medium speed, adding the cold milk and vanilla mixture, a little at a time.

Using a flexible spatula, fold the two mixtures together. Do this very gently so the egg whites do not deflate.

Heat an electric waffle maker to 400°F (200°C). Using a medium-sized ladle, with the capacity of ¾ cup (200 ml) and 4 in. (10 cm) in diameter, pour the mixture into the waffle maker. Wait for 10 seconds before closing the lid.

The cooking time will vary according to the waffle maker you are using, so be patient.

As they cook, dust each waffle generously with confectioners' sugar and serve on hot plates. Add accompaniments of your choice, for example Chantilly cream and grated chocolate.

Hot chocolate

SERVES 8

Prep: 10 min.
(plus infusing the day before,
if appropriate)

· *Scant 3¼ cups (750 ml) whole milk*
· *8 oz. (230 g) Samana ganache*
  bittersweet chocolate, 62% cacao
· *8 oz. (230 g) Carúpano bittersweet*
  chocolate, 70% cacao
· *2¼ oz. (60 g) Tannea milk chocolate,*
  43% cacao
· *Scant 3¼ cups (750 ml) whipping cream*
  from Étrez, 33% butterfat

You can make plain or flavored hot chocolate. If you choose the latter, here are some suggestions for flavoring it:

> *¾ tsp. (4 g) quatre-épices (four spice mix) or ground cinnamon*
> *2 tsp. (10 g) pink peppercorns*
> *1½ tsp. (8 g) tonka bean*
> *Zest of 2 lemons, or 2 clementines, or 1 orange, in strips*
> *Or – very simple – 1 pinch fleur de sel*

For flavored chocolate, prepare the infusion the day before. In a saucepan, bring the milk with your chosen infusion ingredient to a boil. Remove from the heat. Cover, leave to cool and then chill until you are ready to make the hot chocolate. The next day, strain the infused milk through a fine-mesh sieve and bring it briefly to a boil.

For plain hot chocolate, prepare it just before serving.

Chop the chocolates into small pieces. Mix the milk and cream together and bring to a boil. Pour onto the chopped chocolates and blend with an immersion blender. Serve hot.

BRiOCHE

In the words of

FRANÇOIS PERRET

I love the *opulence* of brioche with its reassuring curves and soft, buttery texture. It epitomizes the *aroma* and flavor of breakfast and is a taste from the land of plenty. It evokes so many happy memories for me. It is at the same time very *simple* yet lavish, *plump* yet light, and both an innocent and a *prima donna* at the Ritz Paris' morning feasts. Just see how its roundness makes people's eyes light up! It is also between two worlds, that of the *bakery* and the patisserie, a fine dough that performs a thousand and one gustatory pirouettes. Its airy texture is the realm in which my *imagination* nestles. In this book you will find it in many of my recipes.

SERVES 10

*(makes 2 brioches in 2 loaf pans measuring
3¼ in. × 11 in. (8 cm × 28 cm)
Prep: 1 hr. 30 min. (the dough needs to be
prepared the day before)
Rest: about 2 hr.
Cook: 45 min.*

- ½ oz. (14 g) fresh baker's yeast
- 4 tsp. (20 ml) whole milk
- 4 cups (14 oz./400 g) pastry flour
  (type T45)
- 2¼ tsp. (12 g) fine salt
- Scant ¼ cup (1¾ oz./50 g) brown sugar
- 4 large or 5 small eggs,
  total weight 8 oz. (230 g)
- 1¼ cups (10 oz./280 g) butter
  from Étrez, diced and softened
- 1 egg yolk beaten with a few drops
  of water, for glazing

Crumble the yeast and mix it with the milk to dissolve it. Add the flour, salt, brown sugar, and most of the eggs (set aside 1 egg for 4 cups (14 oz./ 400 g) of flour) Knead in the bowl of a stand mixer fitted with the dough hook on low speed for 10 minutes.

Add the remaining egg and continue to knead on low speed until the dough comes away completely from the sides of the bowl.

Gradually add the butter and knead until the dough comes away from the sides of the bowl again.

Let the dough rest for 1 hour in the refrigerator, in a bowl covered with plastic wrap (cling film). Punch the dough down and fold it over to burst any air bubbles inside. Let it rest again in the refrigerator until the next day, tightly covered in plastic wrap.

The following day, shape 6 balls of dough, each weighing 3 oz. (80 g), and position them in three rows on the diagonal in a loaf pan with the "seam" of each ball underneath on the base of the pan. Tuck the balls against each other so they stick together and press down lightly on the top of each ball to flatten it slightly. Let rise at room temperature until the dough reaches the top of the pan (about 1 hour, depending on the temperature).

Preheat the oven to 300°F (150°C/Gas mark 2). Brush the top of the dough with beaten egg and bake in the oven for 45 minutes.

Brioche

*The quantities given are for making two brioches,
as it is easier to knead a larger quantity of the dough.
Once the brioche is baked, you can freeze it in a hermetically
sealed freezer bag. Defrost at 212°F (100°C).*

Toasted brioche
— *with butter and mirabelles* —
You can adapt this recipe using your favorite fruit.

SERVES 8

Prep: 1 hr. (plus preparing and baking the brioche)
Cook: 2 hr. 15 min.

LA BRIOCHE

· 1 brioche (follow the recipe on page 28 or buy a brioche from your baker or pâtissier)

MIRABELLE JUICE

· 2¼ lb. (1 kg) mirabelles
· Scant ½ cup (3½ oz./100 g) brown sugar

MIRABELLE CHUTNEY

· 4 tbsp. (60 ml) water
· Scant ¼ cup (1¾ oz./50 g) brown sugar
· 1 vanilla bean
· 1½ lb. (720 g) mirabelle flesh (reserved from making the juice)
· 5½ tbsp. (80 ml) mirabelle brandy

TO FINISH

· 1 cup (7 oz./200 g) unsalted butter from Étrez
· 1 lb. 2oz. (500 g) fresh mirabelles
· 3 cups (1 lb. 2 oz./500 g) whole, unskinned almonds
· Fresh thyme sprigs

BRIOCHE

Place the brioche in the freezer for 1 hour to make it easier to slice. If you are not using a toaster, preheat the oven to 275°F (140°C/Gas mark 1). Cut the brioche lengthwise into neat slices, ⅓ in. (8 mm) thick. Trim them, as necessary, to make rectangles. If using a toaster, watch the slices carefully so they do not color too much, or place them between two silicone baking mats and toast in the oven for 10 minutes.

MIRABELLE JUICE

Wash and drain the mirabelles. Cut them in half and remove the pits. Put them in a heatproof mixing bowl and add the sugar. Cover the bowl with plastic wrap (cling film) and heat in a double boiler (bain-marie) for 1 hour. Pass through a fine-mesh sieve and reserve the juice and the mirabelle flesh for the chutney.

MIRABELLE CHUTNEY

In a saucepan on the stove (I use an induction plate), heat the water, brown sugar, and vanilla bean, split with the seeds scraped out and added as well. As soon as the mixture comes to a boil, add the reserved mirabelles. When the mixture is hot, add the brandy and flambé. Let cook for about 5 minutes on medium heat and then for 2 hours on setting 1 on an induction plate. (If using gas or another type of heat: begin with low-medium heat, followed by 2 hours over very low heat, using a heat diffuser if necessary.) When the fruits are soft but still keeping their shape, remove from the heat.
This chutney keeps very well in the refrigerator in a tightly sealed container.

FINISHING AND ASSEMBLING

Remove the butter from the refrigerator at least 1 hour ahead so it comes to room temperature and is not too hard to use. Beat the butter until it is soft and creamy and spoon it into a pastry bag fitted with a fine plain tip, or into a plastic disposable pastry bag and snip off the point to make a small hole.
Cut the mirabelles in half and remove the pits.
Using a sharp knife, cut the almonds lengthwise into slivers.
Pipe the butter in a zigzag pattern on the toasted slices of brioche.
Spread a little of the mirabelle chutney on top and then arrange perfect pieces of mirabelle over the surface (allow about 2 oz. (50 g) mirabelles for each slice).
Decorate with the slivered almonds and small sprigs of thyme. Eat immediately.

MY SWEET TART

In the words of

FRANÇOIS PERRET

When I was growing up, there was never a Sunday when this tart was not on my *family's table*. Its creamy heart, escaping from the generous brioche crust, made my own heart beat impatiently with *anticipation*. As a tribute to my Bressane origins, I wanted to introduce this provincial tart to life in a luxury hotel. Decorating it entirely with a mixture of *sugar and cream*, delighted me. Oh! Crème fraîche, what would my patisserie be without it. It envelops flavors, intensifying them. It is a formidable taste enhancer. As with the milk and butter I use, I have it brought straight from the small dairy cooperative of Étrez in Bresse. It is up to us patisserie chefs to defend the *riches of the French countryside*, its *appellations d'origine protégée* foods, its skilled artisans, and exceptional producers. A return to the best possible ingredients, and healthy creativity that *balances well-being with pleasure*, are both vital to the modern pastry chef.

My sweet Bressane tart

SERVES 10

Prep: 1 hr. 30 min. (the dough must be prepared the day before)
Rest: about 3 hr.
Cook: 45 min.

BRIOCHE DOUGH

· *See recipe page 28*

SWEET GASTRONOMIC CREAM

· *Generous ¾ cup (200 ml) crème gastronomique AOP from Étrez, 40% butterfat*
· *1¼ oz. (50 g) brown sugar*

Prepare the brioche dough (see page 28)

The following day, take the dough out of the refrigerator and work with it while it is still very cold. Put the dough on a silicone baking mat on a baking sheet and roll it out very thinly with a rolling pin, about ⅛ in. (3 mm) thick, to a disk 12 in. (30 cm) in diameter. Prick all over the surface of the dough with a fork and chill it for at least 30 minutes.

Place an 11-in. (28-cm) stainless steel tart ring in the center of the dough and cut around the ring. You can use the excess dough to make other tarts or a brioche. It is necessary to use the quantities of ingredients given for the dough, as this will make the kneading and rising easier.

Preheat the oven to 375°F (190°C/Gas mark 5), ventilated setting.

Just before baking, mix the *crème gastronomique* with the brown sugar, without first whipping the cream, and then carefully pour the mixture onto the disk of dough. Allow about 1 cup (250 ml) for one tart.
Bake the tart in the oven on the silicone baking mat on the baking sheet for 10 minutes.

Citrus "flower show"
— *with Suzette sauce* —

SERVES 8
Prep: 1 hr.

LEMON JELLY
- *3 sheets (6 g) gelatin*
- *¼ pt. (150 ml) water*
- *¼ pt. (150 ml) lemon juice*
- *⅓ cup (2¼ oz./60 g) superfine sugar*

POACHED KUMQUATS
- *11 oz. (300 g) kumquats*
- *2 cups (500 ml) water*
- *Generous 2½ cups (1 lb. 2 oz./500 g) brown sugar*

SUZETTE SAUCE
- *1 tbsp. (½ oz./12 g) potato flour*
- *2¼ tbsp. (35 ml) Grand Marnier*
- *Scant ¾ cup (4½ oz./130 g) superfine sugar*
- *1 cup plus 1 tbsp. (270 ml) orange juice*
- *2 tbsp. (30 ml) lemon juice*
- *2 strips of orange zest*

CANDIED LIME ZEST
- *3 limes*
- *2 cups (500 ml) water and 1¼ cups (9 oz./250 g) sugar (or the kumquat poaching syrup)*

FOR DRESSING THE PLATES
- *3 oranges*
- *2 pink grapefruits*
- *3 limes*
- *Dill, cilantro, and mint leaves*
- *1 fennel bulb (optional)*

MAKE THE LEMON JELLY
Soak the gelatin sheets for 10 minutes in cold water to soften them. Bring the ¼ pt. (150 ml) water to a boil with the lemon juice. Add the sugar and then the squeezed-out gelatin sheets. Divide the jelly between 8 serving plates, making sure there is a ¼-in. (4-mm) thick layer of jelly in each. Cool and then keep chilled.

MAKE THE POACHED KUMQUATS
Using a toothpick, prick each kumquat all the way through from one side to the other. Blanch them four consecutive times in boiling water. Drain. Make a syrup by bringing the 2 cups (500 ml) water and the sugar to a boil. Pour the hot syrup over the kumquats and let cool. Repeat this process as many times as necessary until the kumquats are soft all the way through. Drain the kumquats: you can reserve the syrup to candy the lime zest.

MAKE THE SUZETTE SAUCE
Stir the potato flour and Grand Marnier together until smooth. Reserve. In a saucepan, dissolve the sugar over low heat and then cook it until you have a clear caramel. Deglaze with the citrus juices and add the orange zest. Stir in the flour and Grand Marnier mixture, bring to a boil and pass through a fine-mesh sieve. Cool and then keep chilled.

MAKE THE CANDIED LIME ZEST
Using a vegetable peeler, remove the zest from the limes in strips without removing the white part (the pith). Plunge the zest several times into a saucepan of boiling water. Bring the 2 cups (500 ml) water and the sugar to a boil to make a syrup and then pour this syrup over the lime zest.

DRESS THE PLATES
Using a sharp knife, peel the oranges, grapefruits, and limes. Carefully remove their segments so each one is whole and a perfect shape. Arrange the segments on the serving plates on top of the lemon jelly. Add the candied kumquats, arrange the candied lime zest over them and then decorate generously with dill, cilantro, and small mint leaves. Finish with the Suzette sauce (allowing about 2¼ tbsp. (40 ml) for each plate). You can also add some grated raw fennel.

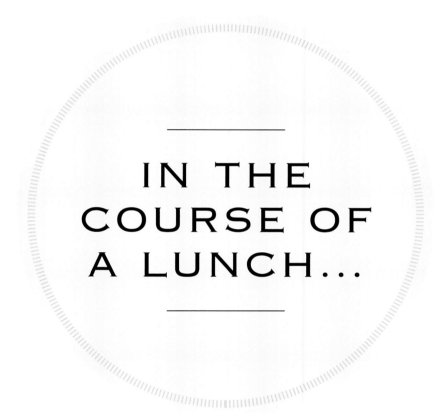

IN THE
COURSE OF
A LUNCH...

In the course of a lunch…

Zacapa rum baba
— *with whipped Étrez cream* —

Why Zacapa rum? For its aromatic and woody fragrance, as to make a good rum baba it is important to use a rum with character.

SERVES 8–10

Prep: 2 hr. (not including rising time)
Soak: 12 hr.

BABA DOUGH
- 1 ⅔ cups (7 oz./200 g) pastry flour (type T45)
- ¾ tsp. (4 g) fine-grain salt
- 5 tsp. (¾ oz./ 20 g) superfine sugar
- ⅓ oz. (10 g) fresh baker's yeast
- Scant ½ cup (100 ml) water
- 2 eggs
- ¼ cup (2¼ oz./60 g) butter at room temperature plus a little extra for the molds

BABA SYRUP
- 4¼ cups (1 liter) water
- 1½ cups (10½ oz./300 g) superfine sugar
- Generous ¾ cup (200 ml) 23-year-old Zacapa rum
- 4 tsp. (20 ml) Grand Marnier

CHANTILLY CREAM
- 1¼ cups (300 ml) whipping cream from Étrez, 33% butterfat
- Generous ¾ cup (200 ml) crème gastronomique from Étrez
- 1¾ oz. (50 g) confectioners' sugar, sifted

GLAZE
- 1 lb. 2 oz. (500 g) clear neutral glaze
- 3½ tbsp. (50 ml) 23-year-old Zacapa rum

TO SERVE
- Generous ¾ cup (200 ml) crème gastronomique from Étrez, 40% butterfat

MAKE THE BABA DOUGH

Put the flour, salt, and sugar in the bowl of a stand mixer fitted with the dough hook attachment. Dissolve the yeast in the water and add to the dry ingredients along with the eggs. Work the dough until it comes away from the sides of the bowl. Cut the butter into pieces and add to the dough, kneading until it comes away from the sides of the bowl again. Lightly and evenly butter small savarin molds and divide the dough between them (about 1 oz./28 g per mold). Leave to rise on a baking sheet for 15–20 minutes. Preheat the oven to 300°F (150°C/Gas mark 2). Place a second baking sheet on top of the molds and bake in the oven for 22 minutes. Unmold the babas and let them dry out in a 250°F (130°C/Gas mark ½) oven for 13 minutes. Arrange the babas in a single layer in a shallow dish.

MAKE THE BABA SYRUP

In a saucepan, bring the water and sugar to a boil and then leave to cool to 122°F (50°C). Add the vanilla bean, rum, and Grand Marnier and pour all the syrup over the babas. Store them overnight in the refrigerator and check that they have absorbed the syrup. Moisten withthe excess syrup, if necessary.

MAKE THE CHANTILLY CREAM

Mix the whipping cream, crème gastronomique, and confectioners' sugar together and whisk until the cream holds its shape. Spoon the cream into a pastry bag fitted with a fluted tip and store in the refrigerator.

ASSEMBLE AND FINISH

Drain the babas. Warm the glaze and brush it over the babas. Pipe a rosette of Chantilly cream into each baba, taking care to leave a space in the center. Fill the center of each baba with *crème gastronomique* from Étrez.

Recipe photographs, following pages.

CHERRY TARTE TATIN

In the words of

FRANÇOIS PERRET

A tarte Tatin is a truly *amazing dessert.* One that evokes all kinds of *emotions.* The way it is cooked concentrates the *fragrance of the fruit* so it becomes mellow but, at the same time it still retains a *little bite,* making it such a pleasure to eat. As if, by *magic,* this tarte has the gift of bringing *fruit to perfect maturity.* And, for me, there is no argument: it is the height of sensuality served warm with crème fraîche. *Thick and slightly acidic* cream for a cherry Tatin, a *sweeter and lighter* one for apples.

In the course of a lunch…

Cherry tarte Tatin
— *with Étrez cream* —

Let your imagination run wild by adapting this recipe using mirabelles, red plums, etc.

SERVES 8

Prep: 3 hr. 30 min.
Cook: 50 min.

CHERRY JUICE
· *2¼ lb. (1 kg) cherries*
· *Scant ½ cup (3½ oz./100 g) brown sugar*

CHERRY CHUTNEY
· *1 Bourbon vanilla bean*
· *Scant ¼ cup (1¾ oz./50 g) brown sugar*
· *4 tbsp. (60 ml) water*
· *1½ lb. (700 g) cherries (the flesh of the cherries from making the juice, plus fresh, pitted cherries to make up the weight)*
· *5 tbsp. (80 ml) kirsch*

STUFFED CHERRIES BAKED IN THE OVEN
· *112 cherries (14 for each tatin)*

MAKE THE CHERRY JUICE

Cut the cherries in half and remove the pits. Put the cherries in a mixing bowl and add the sugar. Cover the bowl with plastic wrap (cling film) and heat it in a bain-marie (water bath) for 1 hour over gentle heat. Strain through a fine-mesh sieve and reserve the juice. Reserve the cherry flesh as well to make the chutney.

MAKE THE CHERRY CHUTNEY

Split the vanilla bean lengthwise and scrape out the seeds. Put the brown sugar, vanilla bean, and seeds in a saucepan on an induction plate and add the water. Bring to a boil and immediately add the cherries. Once the mixture is very hot, add the kirsch and flambé it. Cook for about 5 minutes over medium heat, turn the temperature down to level 1 (or very low) and continue to cook for about 2 hours. When the cherries are a rich, red compote but still keep their shape, remove the saucepan from the heat. Let cool and keep chilled.

MAKE THE STUFFED CHERRIES BAKED IN THE OVEN

Preheat the oven to 325°F (160°C/Gas mark 3). Remove the stalks from the cherries, make a small cut at the base of each one and remove the pits without spoiling the shape of the fruit. Fill each cherry with chutney and then stand all the stuffed cherries in 8 molds, 4 in. (10 cm) in diameter, and cover with aluminum foil. Cook them in the oven for about 20 minutes. When they come out of the oven, carefully rearrange the cherries in the molds into circles, 3¼ in. (8 cm) in diameter.

BRETON SHORTBREAD PASTRY

· ⅓ cup (3¼ oz./90 g) lightly salted
  butter, softened
· ⅔ cup (3¼ oz./90 g)
  confectioners' sugar
· 2 egg yolks
· 1 cup plus 1 tbsp. (4½ oz./130 g)
  all-purpose flour and ½ tsp. (2 g)
  baking powder, sifted together

CHERRY SAUCE

· ¾ tsp. (3 g) potato flour
· Generous ¾ cup (200 ml)
  cherry juice

TO SERVE

· 1 cup (240 ml) crème gastronomique
  from Étrez AOP
· Cambodian Kampot red pepper
  in a pepper mill

MAKE THE BRETON SHORTBREAD PASTRY

Preheat the oven to 325°F (160°C/Gas mark 3). Using a stand mixer fitted with the paddle beater, slowly beat the butter and confectioners' sugar together and then add the egg yolks. Incorporate the sifted flour and baking powder. It is very important not to emulsify the dough: it must be prepared on very low speed.

Roll out the pastry ¼ in. (4.5 mm) thick and, using tart rings, ⅓ in (8 cm) in diameter, cut out 8 disks. Lightly butter the insides of the rings before placing them on a baking sheet and putting the pastry disks inside. Bake in the oven for 10–15 minutes.

MAKE THE CHERRY SAUCE

Using a flexible spatula (not a whisk), mix the potato flour with 4 tsp (20 ml) cherry juice. Heat the rest of the juice and, when it is very hot (but not boiling), add the flour and cherry juice mixture, stirring gently and letting the mixture boil for 3 minutes. Strain through a fine-mesh sieve, leave to cool and keep chilled.

TO SERVE

Just before serving, lightly whip the cream until it holds soft peaks.

Place each cherry tatin on a round of Breton pastry. Reheat in the oven at 350°F (180°C/Gas mark 4) for 4 minutes and then brush a thin layer of sauce over each tatin. Give two turns of red pepper from the mill over the cherries, add a big spoonful of lightly whipped cream and finish by pouring the sauce over in front of your guests.

Recipe photograph, following page.

Tarte Tatin

Don't limit yourself to just making the tart with apples as you could use mangoes, peaches, quinces… But, take care, as the cooking time will be different for each fruit.

SERVES 8

Prep: 1 hr.
Cook: 2 hr. 15 min.

BRETON SHORTBREAD PASTRY
· *⅔ cup (3 oz./80 g) all-purpose flour*
· *½ tsp. (2 g) baking powder*
· *Scant ½ cup (3½ oz./100 g) butter, softened*
· *⅓ cup (1½ oz./40 g) confectioners' sugar*
· *¼ cup (¾ oz./20 g) ground almonds*
· *1 tbsp. (¾ oz./20 g) egg yolk*

CARAMEL AND APPLE FILLING
· *Lightly salted butter (for the pan)*
· *½ cup (4 oz./110 g) superfine sugar*
· *4 lb. (1.8 kg) apples (about 9 apples), peeled weight*

IMBIBING SAUCE FOR BAKING
· *3½ tbsp. (1¾ oz./50 g) butter*
· *1 tbsp. (15 ml) calvados*
· *2½ tsp. (10 g) superfine sugar*

MAKE THE BRETON SHORTBREAD PASTRY
Preheat the oven to 325°F (160°C/Gas mark 3). Sift the flour with the baking powder. Beat together the softened butter, confectioners' sugar, and ground almonds and then add the egg yolks and finally the sifted flour and baking powder. Line a baking sheet with parchment paper. Transfer the dough to a pastry bag fitted with a plain, no. 12 tip (⅓ in. (8 mm) in diameter) and pipe it in a spiral measuring 8 ½ in. (22 cm) in diameter, starting at the center. Bake in the oven for 10–12 minutes, watching it carefully to ensure the pastry does not color too much.

MAKE THE CARAMEL AND APPLE FILLING
Butter a 11–11½ in. (28–29 cm) plain, round copper cake pan about 2½ in. (6 cm deep), and line with a disk of parchment paper of the same size. Butter the paper as well.

Cook the sugar over a low heat until it dissolves and becomes an auburn-colored caramel and has almost reached smoking point, and then pour it into the copper pan.

Peel and core the apples and cut each one into 6 segments. Arrange them as flat as possible over the caramel in the copper pan, packing them tightly together.

MAKE THE IMBIBING SAUCE FOR BAKING
Heat the ingredients together over a low heat until the butter and sugar are just melted, without letting them cook. Brush the mix twice all over the apples.

Recipe photograph, previous page.

CALVADOS GLAZE
· ½ vanilla bean
· 10½ oz. (300 g) clear neutral glaze
· 2 tbsp. (30 ml) calvados

TO SERVE
· Crème gastronomique *from Étrez,*
  40% butterfat

BAKE THE TATIN
Preheat the oven to 325°F (160°C/Gas mark 3).

Before putting the tatin in the oven, brush the apples again with the imbibing sauce. Place in the oven and wait until the juice has settled at the bottom of the pan. Carefully spoon off the juice and reserve it. Brush over a new layer of imbibing sauce and put the tatin back in the oven for 45 minutes.

At the end of this time, spoon off the juice again and add to the previously reserved juice. Using a brush, re-moisten the apples with the collected juice. Cover with a sheet of aluminum foil and return to the oven for 45 minutes.

Spoon off the juice once more and moisten the apples again with it. Replace the foil and bake for an additional 30 minutes. Check to see the tatin is cooked as the timing can vary depending on the variety of apple used: the apples must be a beautiful uniform red-gold color. Stand the pan on a cold baking sheet to prevent further cooking and leave to cool without removing the foil.

When the apples are completely cold, use an angled spatula to gently press them down and make the surface level. Keep in the refrigerator.

ASSEMBLE AND FINISH
Heat all the ingredients for the calvados glaze. Neaten the shortbread pastry around the apples.

To unmold the tatin, heat the base of the pan directly over a gas flame or with a blow torch, then turn the tatin upside down and unmold onto a serving plate. Brush with the calvados glaze and serve accompanied with *crème gastronomique* from Étrez.

CRISP
MERINGUE

In the words of

FRANÇOIS PERRET

The *gourmand* that I am demands abundance and my eyes light up at the sight of a dessert. It has to be *huge*! From the beginning, this passion told me that I was not going to miss out, that my *pleasure* was not going to be diminished by parsimony. But generous servings must go hand in hand with *total lightness*. It's what I like so much about meringue: it is the *hot-air balloon* of patisserie. With this dessert, which was created for Les Jardins de L'Espadon restaurant, I wanted something very *pure*, very *white*, and very *airy*. And, at the same time, the powerful attraction of chocolate draws the *spoon* to the plate where it happily scoops up the sauce.

In the course of a lunch…

Crisp meringue
— *with melting Carúpano chocolate* —

SERVES 8

Prep: 2 hr. (it is best to make the chocolate sauce the day before)
Cook: 1 hr. 20 min.

CHOCOLATE CRÉMEUX
- ½ cup (140 ml) whole milk
- 1¾ oz. (50 g) Tannea milk chocolate 43% cacao
- 1¾ oz. (50 g) Carúpano bittersweet chocolate 70% cacao
- 3¼ tbsp. (1½ oz./40 g) brown sugar
- ¼ cup (2¼ oz./60 g) egg yolk (3 medium yolks)
- ½ cup (130 ml) whipping cream from Étrez, 33% butterfat, well-chilled

CARÚPANO CHOCOLATE SAUCE
- 2½ oz. (70 g) Carúpano bittersweet chocolate, 70% cacao
- ⅓ oz. (10 g) Tannea milk chocolate, 43% cacao
- ½ cup (120 ml) UHT single cream
- ½ cup (120 ml) whole milk

MAKE THE CHOCOLATE CRÉMEUX

In a saucepan, bring the milk to a boil, remove it from the heat and reserve.

Break the chocolates into small pieces and put them in a large bowl. Whisk the sugar and egg yolks until thick and pale. Make a crème anglaise by pouring the milk gradually onto the sugar and yolks, whisking constantly, and then stir in a saucepan over medium heat. When the crème anglaise has thickened, pour it onto the chocolates, blending with an immersion blender. Add the well-chilled cream, mix with a pastry scraper and then blend again. Cool the crémeux quickly and keep chilled.

MAKE THE CARÚPANO CHOCOLATE SAUCE

Prepare this the day before if possible. Break the chocolates into small pieces and put them in a large bowl. In a saucepan, bring the cream and milk to a boil, pour onto the chocolates in two equal amounts. Blend with an immersion blender and then keep chilled.

MAKE THE MI-CUITE MERINGUE

Preheat the oven to 200°F (90°C/Gas on lowest setting). Whisk the egg whites until stiff, adding the superfine sugar as they start to thicken. When they are very firm, fold in the confectioners' sugar and some of the chopped cacao nibs, using a flexible spatula. Spoon the meringue into a pastry bag fitted with a plain no. 8 tip and pipe the meringue into domes, 1⅓ in. (3.5 cm) in diameter, onto a parchment sheet lined with baking paper. Dust them with more chopped cacao nibs. Bake for 20 minutes in the oven and then turn each dome over and scrape out the center using a small spoon (regularly rinsed in water), preserving the shell. Return the shells to the oven for a further 1 hour.

In the course of a lunch…

MI-CUITE MERINGUE

- ½ cup (4 oz./120 g) egg white (4 medium whites)
- Generous ½ cup (4½ oz./120 g) superfine sugar
- Scant 1 cup (4 oz./120 g) confectioners' sugar, sifted
- Cacao nibs, finely chopped

BLANCMANGE

- 1 pinch (1 g) powdered gelatin
- ⅔ cup (5¼ oz./150 g) egg white (5 medium whites)
- ½ cup (4 oz./110 g) superfine sugar

CHOCOLATE CURLS

- 9 oz. (250 g) Carúpano bittersweet chocolate, 70% cacao

MAKE THE BLANCMANGE

Hydrate the gelatin in a little cold water for 10 minutes and then dissolve it in a microwave.

Whisk the egg whites with the sugar to soft peaks. Add the melted gelatin and whisk again briefly. Transfer the blancmange to a pastry bag fitted with a plain no. 12 tip and pipe it into domes, 1⅜ in. (3.5 cm) in diameter, and finishing in a point, on a baking sheet lined with parchment paper. Cook for 3 minutes at 176°F (80°C) in a steam oven or in a steamer on gentle heat.

MAKE THE CHOCOLATE CURLS

To temper the chocolate: melt it and heat to around 122°F (50°C) and then quickly lower the temperature to 81°F (27°C) (it is important the temperature does not fall below this). Gently heat the chocolate again to liquify it, so it reaches a maximum temperature of 88–90°F (31–32°C).

Using a spatula, spread the chocolate over a marble slab or other flat, cold surface. Leave it to set and then, using the blade of a knife or a triangular paint scraper, shave curls off the chocolate.

ASSEMBLY

Pour a pool of chocolate sauce in the center of 8 soup plates. Fill the meringues with the crémeux, taking care to make the tops beautifully rounded. Finish by adding the blancmange and 3 chocolate curls to each, positioning them attractively. Repeat three times (3 meringues per serving). Arrange the meringues in a star and serve.

Recipe photograph, following page.

CHOCOLATE
CAKE

In the words of

FRANÇOIS PERRET

What could be better at *bringing people together* than a chocolate cake… Here is a recipe that is easy, works well, and is *almost homely.* Accompanied with the rich egg custard crème anglaise, it is a classic on the chalkboards of Parisian brasseries. I have not added any flour to the cake batter. Not because it's the fashionable thing to do but more through loyalty to my philosophy of *visual abundance* and inherent lightness, achieved by increased volume. As for the crème anglaise, it is the *reason for my vocation* as a pâtissier. What was amazing and so good is that it was *my father* who pushed me into wanting to unlock the alchemy that took place in cooking pans. How could anyone succeed in making something so *wonderful*? For me, my *father's* crème anglaise will never be *equaled.* And for this I owe him a lot.

Flourless chocolate cake
— *with crème anglaise* —

SERVES 8–10

Prep: 1 hr.
Rest: 12 hr. for the vanilla infusion;
allow 3–4 hr. for freezing
Cook: 45 min.

TRADITIONAL CRÈME ANGLAISE
· *1 vanilla bean*
· *5½ cups (1.3 liters) whole milk*
· *Scant 1 cup (5½ oz./160 g)*
  brown sugar
· *1¼ cups (11½ oz./320 g) egg yolk*
  (about 16 medium yolks)

FLOURLESS CHOCOLATE CAKE
· *3½ oz. (100 g) Carúpano bittersweet*
  chocolate, 70% cacao
· *2¼ oz. (60 g) cacao paste*
· *Generous 1 cup (10½ oz./290 g)*
  egg yolk (about 15 medium yolks)
· *Generous 1 cup (8½ oz./240 g)*
  egg white (8 medium whites)
· *1 cup (7 oz./200 g) brown sugar*

MAKE THE TRADITIONAL CRÈME ANGLAISE

The day before, prepare the vanilla infusion. Cut the vanilla bean into small pieces. In a saucepan, bring half the milk to a boil with the vanilla, blending with an immersion blender. Remove from the heat, add the rest of the milk and cover. When cool, let infuse overnight in the refrigerator.

The next day, strain the milk through a fine-mesh sieve and top up with extra milk to the original quantity. Bring to a simmer. Whisk the sugar and egg yolks together until pale and creamy, whisk in the milk and then cook, stirring constantly with a spatula, until the temperature reaches 180°F (82°C) and the mixture coats the spatula so that when a line is drawn through it, the line does not close up again. Strain at once through a fine-mesh sieve, cover and place immediately in the refrigerator.

MAKE THE FLOURLESS CHOCOLATE CAKE

Preheat the oven to 300°F (150°C/Gas mark 2). Melt the chocolate and cacao paste in a bain-marie (water bath) to 104°F (40°C).

In a stand mixer fitted with the whisk attachment, beat the egg yolks and egg whites with the sugar until light and mousse-like. Switch off the mixer and, using a flexible spatula, incorporate the melted chocolate into the whisked egg mixture. Place a silicone baking mat on a baking sheet, stand a baking frame measuring 9 × 9 in. (23 × 23 cm) and 1¾ in. (4.5 cm) high on the mat and pour the mixture into it. Bake in the oven for about 45 minutes. Let cool and then trim the top of the cake so that it is flat and the cake 1⅜ in. (3.5 cm) is high.

In the course of a lunch...

CHOCOLATE MOUSSE

· 5 oz. (150 g) Carúpano bittersweet
  chocolate, 70% cacao
· ½ cup (130 ml) whipping cream
· ⅓ cup (3 oz./80 g) egg yolk
  (about 4 large yolks)
· ¾ oz. (20 g) superfine sugar
  for the egg yolks
· 2½ tsp. (10 g) superfine sugar
  for the egg whites
· Generous ½ cup (4½ oz./130 g egg
  white) (4 large whites)

DARK CHOCOLATE ICING

· 3 sheets (6 g) gelatin
· Scant 1 cup (210 ml) UHT
  single cream
· Scant 1 cup (200 ml)
  whole milk
· ¾ cup (4½ oz./155 g) superfine sugar
· 1¾ oz. (50 g) unsweetened
  cocoa powder
· 2 oz. (55 g) Tannea milk chocolate,
  43% cacao

MAKE THE CHOCOLATE MOUSSE

Melt the chocolate in a bain-marie to 122°F (50°C). Lightly whip the cream so it is standing in soft but not firm peaks. Keep chilled in the refrigerator.

Beat the egg yolks with the ¾ oz. (20 g) sugar (until they are light and have the texture of a sabayon). Meanwhile, whisk the whites to soft peaks and then stiffen them by whisking in the 2½ tsp. (10 g) sugar but, do this carefully, as the whites must not be too firm.

Mix the melted chocolate with half the whipped cream and then immediately add to half the egg whites and half the egg yolk sabayon. Begin by whisking the mixtures together and finish by using a flexible spatula. Fold in the rest of the whipped cream, the remaining whisked whites and the sabayon. Keep chilled.

MAKE THE DARK CHOCOLATE ICING

Soak the gelatin sheets in cold water for 10 minutes. Heat the cream, milk, and sugar together in a saucepan. When boiling, stir in the cocoa powder. Chop the chocolate, pour the hot cream mixture onto it and add the squeezed-out gelatin sheets. Process with an immersion blender and then strain through a fine-mesh sieve. Use this icing when it cools to 104°F (40°C).

ASSEMBLE AND DECORATE

Lay the flourless chocolate cake in a baking frame, 1⅓ in. (4.5 cm) deep. Spread chocolate mousse over the cake, smoothing it in an even layer with a spatula. Transfer to the freezer. Reserve the remaining mousse for spreading over other desserts. Freeze if necessary.

Cut the frozen dessert into strips, 4½ in. (11 cm) long and 1½ in. (4 cm) wide. Ice each strip with the dark chocolate icing. You can also leave the cake whole: protect the sides with an acetate strip and then apply the icing. Serve with the crème anglaise.

Recipe photograph, page 57.

SERVES 8

Prep: 1 hr. 30 min.
Cook: 3 min.

POACHED RHUBARB
· 2¼ lb. (1 kg) rhubarb
· 4¼ cups (1 liter) water
· 1 cup (7 oz./200 g) superfine sugar
· Grenadine syrup, for color

OPALINE SUGAR TUILES
· 3¾ oz. (110 g) fondant
· 2½ oz. (75 g) glucose syrup
· Pink peppercorns

YOGURT SORBET
· ⅔ cup (150 ml) UHT
  whole milk
· 1 Bourbon vanilla bean
· 6 tbsp. (90 ml) UHT whipping cream
· Scant 1 cup (5½ oz./160 g)
  superfine sugar
· 2¼ cups (19 oz./550 g)
  strained plain yogurt

TO FINISH
· 1 bunch fresh chives
· 1 bunch flat-leaf parsley

MAKE THE POACHED RHUBARB
Wash and dry the rhubarb. Cut it into batons of different lengths and place in a shallow dish.

In a saucepan, bring the water and sugar to a boil with just enough grenadine syrup to obtain the color of your choice. Pour the hot syrup onto the batons of rhubarb and let cool completely. Drain the rhubarb, reserving the syrup. Check that the rhubarb is tender all the way through (it must keep its shape). If it is not completely tender, bring the syrup back to a boil and pour it over the rhubarb again. Repeat this operation until the rhubarb is poached but still keeps its shape.

MAKE THE OPALINE SUGAR TUILES
Heat the fondant and the glucose to 329°C (165°C). Pour the mixture onto a silicone baking mat and leave it to cool completely in a dry place. Blend it to a powder, continuing to keep it dry. Preheat the oven to 350°F (180°C/Gas mark 4). Place three different-sized round stencils (½ in., ¾ in., and 1¼ in / 1 cm, 2 cm, and 3 cm) on a silicone baking mat on a baking sheet and dust the stencils with a thin and even layer of the powder. Crush the pink peppercorns onto the layer of sugar dust before cooking in the oven for 3 minutes. Remove from the oven and leave to cool.

MAKE THE YOGURT SORBET
In a saucepan, bring the milk to a boil. Split the vanilla bean lengthwise and add to the hot milk with the scraped-out seeds. Remove from the heat and leave to infuse for 10 minutes. Remove the vanilla bean, add the cream and the sugar and bring to a boil. Pour the mixture over the yogurt and blend it first on low speed and then on turbo.

ASSEMBLE
Stand lengths of rhubarb up in each serving plate, in an irregular pattern, spooning over a little of the syrup. Add some small quenelles of yogurt sorbet, the opaline pink peppercorn sugar tuiles, and decorate with chive stems and parsley sprigs.

Rhubarb with herbs
— yogurt, and pink peppercorns —

AFTERNOON
TEA REGAINED

Teddy bear

— *marshmallows* —

SERVES 8

Prep: 1 hr.
Rest: 24 hr, plus 1 hr. for the pastry
Cook: 10 min.

LEMON MARSHMALLOW

· 3½ leaves (7 g) gelatin
· 1 cup (7½ oz./210 g) superfine sugar
· 4 tsp. (¾ oz./20 g) glucose syrup
· 2½ tbsp. (40 ml) water
· 4 tbsp. (2 oz./60 g) egg white
  (2 medium whites)
· Finely grated zest of 5 lemons

SWEET PASTRY

· ⅔ cup (5¼ oz./150 g) butter, softened,
  plus a little to grease the tart ring
· ⅔ cup (3 oz./90 g) confectioners' sugar
· 1 oz. (30 g) ground almonds
· 1 egg
· 1 pinch (1 g) fleur de sel
· Seeds of ½ vanilla bean
· 2 cups (9 oz./250 g) all-purpose flour

MAKE THE LEMON MARSHMALLOW

Soak the gelatin for 10 minutes in cold water. Lightly oil a 9-in. (23-cm) square baking frame, about 3/8 in. (1 cm) deep, and place it on a baking sheet lined with parchment paper. In a saucepan, heat the sugar, liquid glucose, and water to 248°F (120°C). Squeeze out the gelatin and dissolve it in the syrup.

In a stand mixer fitted with the whisk attachment, whisk the egg whites to firm peaks. Keeping the motor running, pour the syrup into the whisked whites in a thin stream. Continue whisking for 10–12 minutes and then, using a flexible spatula, incorporate the lemon zest. Scrape into the baking frame and let rest for 24 hours.

MAKE THE SWEET PASTRY

In the stand mixer, beat the butter with the confectioners' sugar and ground almonds. Add the egg, fleur de sel, and vanilla seeds. Sift the flour and lightly work it into the mixture to make a smooth dough. Wrap it in plastic wrap (cling film) and let rest for 1 hour in the refrigerator.

Preheat the oven to 325°F (160°C/Gas mark 3). Using a rolling pin, roll out the pastry as thinly as possible, (1 mm), thick and, with a teddy bear cutter, 2½ in. (6 cm) tall, cut out 16 shapes. As you cut them out, lay the shapes on a silicone baking mat placed on a baking sheet. Bake in the oven for about 10 minutes.

ASSEMBLY

Cut out 8 teddy bear shapes from the marshmallow using the same cutter you used for the pastry, or use another shape of cutter of your choice (in which case the same cutter must be used for the pastry). Sit a marshmallow teddy bear on a pastry teddy bear and cover with another pastry bear.

HONEY MADELEINES

In the words of

FRANÇOIS PERRET

As a tribute to the author of *In Search of Lost Time*, this madeleine is part of the *"thé à la française"* (French afternoon tea) that I have introduced in the Salon Proust, an *intimate setting* for afternoons at the Ritz Paris. There is actually no need for me to search across the Channel for ideas to create delicacies for this *timeless occasion*, as France also has its own incomparable recipes. To start with, we are *exceptional bakers* and this little cake, shaped like a scallop shell, has become the stuff of legend. Also, when I was cocooned in a library, where nothing could disturb me, I became fascinated by the abundance of choice that lets everyone discover their madeleine, recalling happy memories *of smell and taste* embedded since *childhood.* And, of course, everything begins and ends with a madeleine. First, when swallowed with a drop of lemon-infused milk, it is only a mouthful. And, finally, there is this gilded sugar madeleine that is soft, *crisp* but melt-in-the-mouth, almost comfort food, where I let you into the secret of double baking.

Honey madeleines

SERVES 8-10

Prep: 30 min.
Rest: ideally 2 days; if not, 24 hr.
Cook: 10–12 min.

MADELEINE BATTER

· 1¾ cups (5½ oz./160 g) pastry
  flour (type T45)
· 2 tsp. (10 g) baking powder
· ⅔ cup (5½ oz./160 g) butter, plus
  extra for the madeleine baking tray
· 3 eggs at room temperature
· ½ cup (3½ oz./100 g) superfine
  sugar
· 1½ oz. (40 g) acacia honey
· 1 oz. (30 g) chestnut honey

ICING

· 1½ cups (10 oz./300 g)
  confectioners' sugar
· 4¾ tbsp. (70 ml) water
· 1 tsp. (5 g) ascorbic acid
· 2½ tbsp. (40 ml) olive oil

MAKE THE MADELEINE BATTER

Sift the flour with the baking powder. Melt the butter. In a stand mixer fitted with the paddle beater, mix the eggs with the sugar and the two honeys. Gradually mix in the sifted flour and baking powder. Finally add the melted, hot butter. Once the batter is made, switch off the mixer to avoid it emulsifying. Chill the batter in the refrigerator for at least 24 hours before using. The next day, butter a madeleine baking tray. Preheat the oven to 350°F (180°C/Gas mark 4).

Divide the batter between the cups in the tray and place it in the oven. Lower the temperature to 325°F (160°C/Gas mark 3) and bake the madeleines for 10–12 minutes until they are golden.

You can eat them on the day they are made but it is better to bake them the day before. Once the madeleines are cold, wrap them in plastic wrap (cling film) and let rest before icing the next day.

MAKE THE ICING

Preheat the oven to 400–425°F (200–220°C/Gas mark 6–7).

Mix the ingredients for the icing together.

Brush the icing over the madeleines and bake them in the oven for about 2 minutes until the icing is dry to the touch. Serve warm or at room temperature.

Afternoon tea regained

Vanilla chouquettes

You can fill the chouquettes with crème pâtissière or even Chantilly cream. This is how to make your own vanilla powder: when you have used a vanilla bean for another recipe, dry it and then grind it to a powder. Sift and reserve the fine powder, storing it in a tightly sealed container.

SERVES 8
(makes about 40 chouquettes)
Prep: 30 min.
Cook: 30 min.

· 1 cup (8½ oz./240 g) egg
  (about 5 medium eggs)
· 1 cup plus scant ½ cup
  (6 oz./170 g) all-purpose flour
· ½ cup (140 ml) milk
· ½ cup (140 ml) water
· ½ cup (4 oz./110 g) butter, diced
· 1 tsp. (5 g) sugar
· 1 tsp. (5 g) salt
· 2 tsp. (10 g) vanilla powder,
  plus a little for dusting
· Brown sugar for dusting

Preheat the oven to 350°F (180°C/Gas mark 4). Whisk the eggs and sift the flour. In a saucepan, heat the milk, water, butter, sugar, and salt. When boiling, add the flour and vanilla powder, stirring with a spatula. Mix until the dough comes away completely from the sides of the saucepan. Transfer to the bowl of a stand mixture fitted with the whisk attachment and beat in the eggs, a little at a time, until the choux batter holds its shape—you may need to adjust the quantity of egg you add to obtain the correct consistency.

Spoon the choux batter into a pastry bag fitted with a smooth no. 12 tip and pipe rounds of choux, 1½ in. (4 cm) in diameter, onto a baking sheet lined with parchment paper. Dust immediately with brown sugar, taking care to cover the surface of each choux round completely. Remove the excess brown sugar by tapping the baking sheet.

Immediately place in the oven and bake for about 30 minutes. When the choux come out of the oven, dust them with vanilla powder, sifting it over the buns using a small sieve.

SERVES 8

Prep: 30 min.
Cook: 30 min. (not including time for making the conserve)

SPONGE CAKE
- ⅓ cup (3½ oz./100 g) egg yolk (about 5 yolks)
- 1 egg white, plus ½ cup (4 oz./110 g) egg white (about 4 whites)
- ½ cup (2¼ oz./60 g) confectioners' sugar
- 1 g vanilla powder
- Finely grated zest of 1 lemon
- ⅓ cup (2¼ oz./60 g) superfine sugar
- 1 cup (4 oz./120 g) all-purpose flour, sifted
- Butter and flour for the silicone baking mat

- **ICING (Christophe Michalak's recipe)**
- 2⅓ cups (10½ oz./300 g) confectioners' sugar
- 5 tbsp. (80 ml) lemon juice
- 2½ tbsp. (40 ml) olive oil

TO FINISH
- 4½ oz. (130 g) raspberry conserve (see recipe, page 160)

MAKE THE SPONGE CAKE

Preheat the oven to 325°F (160°C/Gas mark 3).

In a stand mixture fitted with the whisk attachment, beat together the egg yolks, 1 egg white, confectioners' sugar, vanilla powder, and lemon zest until pale and mousse-like.

In another bowl, whisk the ½ cup (4 oz./110 g) egg white until stiff, adding the superfine sugar in two equal amounts, and continuing to whisk until the whites are firm but not grainy.

Using a flexible spatula, gently fold the egg yolk mixture and the whisked whites together. Finally, fold in the sifted flour.

Butter and flour a cake ring, 8 in. (20 cm) in diameter and 2 in. (5 cm) deep, and also a silicone baking mat placed on a baking sheet. Put the cake ring on the silicone mat and spoon the cake batter into it so it is three-quarters full. Bake in the oven for 28–30 minutes. Take the cake out of the oven and transfer it from the baking sheet to a wire rack (still on the silicone mat) to prevent further cooking. Wait for 5 minutes and then unmold the cake onto the rack. Do not leave it to cool in the ring.

ASSEMBLE AND FINISH

Mix the ingredients for the icing together. Preheat the oven to 425°F (220°C/Gas mark 7).

Using a serrated knife, cut the sponge cake in half horizontally and sandwich the two halves together with the raspberry conserve. Brush the icing over the cake and return it to the oven for 2 minutes.

Raspberry gateau

You can make this cake using other conserves such as apricot, strawberry, cherry…

Florentines

SERVES 8

Prep: 1 hr. 30 min.
Cook: 17 min.

FLORENTINE MIXTURE
- *1 oz. (30 g) candied bigarreaux cherries*
- *1 oz. (30 g) candied orange peel*
- *A little flour for the candied fruits*
- *¾ cup (170 ml) whipping cream*
- *½ cup (3½ oz./100 g) superfine sugar*
- *4 tsp. (¾ oz./20 g) glucose syrup 40*
- *1½ tbsp. (1 oz./30 g) acacia honey*
- *1½ tsp. (10 g) chestnut honey*
- *¼ cup (2¼ oz./60 g) butter*
- *¾ cup (4½ oz./120 g) slivered almonds*
- *⅓ cup (1½ oz./40 g) all-purpose flour*

SHORTCRUST PASTRY
- *Scant ¾ cup (3 oz./80 g) lightly salted butter, softened*
- *Generous ⅓ cup (1¾ oz./50 g) confectioners' sugar*
- *1 egg yolk*
- *1 cup plus 1 tbsp. (5 oz./140 g) all-purpose flour*
- *¼ cup (¾ oz./20 g) ground almonds*

TO FINISH
9 oz. (250 g) Carúpano bittersweet chocolate, 70% cacao, chopped

MAKE THE FLORENTINE MIXTURE

Chop the candied cherries and cut the candied orange peel into small dice. Dust both with flour, shaking them in a sieve to remove the excess flour.

In a saucepan and using an instant-read thermometer, heat the cream, sugar, glucose syrup, honeys, and butter to 226°F (108°C). Add the slivered almonds, chopped candied cherries, and cubes of orange peel and, finally, the flour.

Roll out the dough to a thickness of ⅛ in. (3 mm) between two sheets of parchment paper. Freeze until firm and then cut the dough into squares using a 9-in. (23-cm) square baking frame.

MAKE THE SHORTCRUST PASTRY

Preheat the oven to 325°F (170°C/Gas mark 3), ventilated setting. In the bowl of a stand mixer, beat the butter until creamy. Add, in the following order, the sugar, egg yolk, flour, and ground almonds and mix to make a smooth dough.

Roll out the dough 1/16 in. (1.5 mm) thick using a rolling mill for patisserie or a rolling pin. Cut it into 9-in. (23-cm) squares (the same size as the Florentine squares), place on a silicone baking mat and bake blind in the oven for 7 minutes. Let cool.

TO FINISH

Place the pastry bases in lightly buttered 9 in. (23 cm) baking frames and lift the Florentine squares on top. Bake in the oven for 10 minutes at 325°F (170°C/Gas mark 3). Leave to cool slightly, unmold, and then turn the squares over, carefully neaten the edges, and then cut the squares into ¾ × 4½ in. (2 × 11 cm) bars using a serrated knife.

Melt the chocolate in a bain-marie until the temperature reaches 122°F (50°C) on an instant-read thermometer. Remove the chocolate from the bain-marie and, dipping the bottom of the bowl in cold water, quickly reduce the temperature of the chocolate throughout to 81°C (27°C), not just the temperature of it at the bottom of the bowl. Replace the bowl in the bain-marie to liquify the chocolate and reheat it to a maximum of 88–90°F (31–32°C). Dip the pastry side of the florentines in the tempered chocolate. Leave to cool and set on a wire rack.

Chocolate soufflé meringues

SERVES 8

Prep: 1 hr.
Cook: 1 hr. 40 min.

FRENCH MERINGUE

· 1⅓ cups (10½ oz./300 g) egg white
  (about 10 whites)
· 2⅓ cups (1 lb./450 g) superfine sugar

CHOCOLATE COATING

· 9 oz. (250 g) Carúpano bittersweet
  chocolate, 70% cacao, chopped

MAKE THE FRENCH MERINGUE

Preheat the oven to 225°F (110°C/Gas mark ¼). Whisk the egg whites to firm peaks and then gradually whisk in the sugar to make a stiff meringue. Heat it a little with a blow torch. Spoon the meringue into a pastry bag fitted with a plain tip and pipe into mounds, 2 in. (5 cm) in diameter, onto a baking sheet lined with parchment paper. Cook the meringues in the oven for 30 minutes, keeping the oven door very slightly open, for example, by using the handle of a spoon to prevent it from closing completely. Lower the temperature to 190°F (90°C/Gas on lowest setting) and cook for 1 hour 10 minutes with the oven door closed. Keep in a dry place, protecting the meringues from moisture.

MAKE THE CHOCOLATE COATING

Melt the chocolate in a bain-marie until the temperature reaches 122°F (50°C) on an instant-read thermometer. Remove the chocolate from the bain-marie and, dipping the bottom of the bowl in cold water, quickly reduce the temperature of the chocolate throughout to 81°C (27°C), not just the temperature of it at the bottom of the bowl. Replace the bowl in the bain-marie to liquify the chocolate and reheat it to a maximum of 88–90°F (31–32°C). Spoon the chocolate into a disposable plastic pastry bag but do not snip off the point until you are ready to decorate the meringues.

TO FINISH

Put the meringues on a wire rack with a sheet of parchment paper or a silicone baking mat underneath. Snip off the point of the pastry bag containing the chocolate to make a small hole and pipe it over the meringues. Tap the wire rack smartly to remove excess chocolate and finish coating the meringues. Using an angled spatula, transfer the meringues immediately to a sheet of parchment paper or a silicone baking mat and let the chocolate set.

FIG TART

In the words of

FRANÇOIS PERRET

This tart recalls the *sunny days of my childhood.* The compote of fresh apricots that my mother filled it with, before adding a row of *luscious apricot halves,* created an intoxicating contrast between the mellow fruit and the crisp pastry. Today, I adapt my secret passion for *my mother's recipe* to suit the seasons. It works wonderfully well with figs. Generally speaking, I like the freshness that fruits bring to a dessert. Their juice *lightens the sugar* and the fat, and fruits also have this natural beauty that needs no "wow factors" to catch the eye and make *the mouth water.* In patisserie they add the *flavor and fragrance* of gardens, orchards, and berries gathered by the side of the road... Fruits are part of the fundamental flavors that make up our *taste palate.*

My mother's fig tart

SERVES 8–10

Prep: 1 hr.
Rest: 1 hr. for the pastry (prepare the fig filling the day before)
Cook: 20 min.

FIG COMPOTE
- *4 tbsp. (60 ml) thick (heavy) cream from Étrez*
- *Scant 1 cup (7 oz./200 g) brown sugar*
- *3 eggs*
- *Scant ½ cup (100 ml) gin*
- *3 oz. (80 g) fresh figs*

PASTRY FOR THE TARTLET SHELLS
- *⅓ cup (3 oz./80 g) lightly salted butter, softened*
- *Generous ⅓ cup (1¾ oz./50 g) confectioners' sugar*
- *1 egg yolk*
- *1 cup plus 1 tbsp. (5 oz./140 g) all-purpose flour*
- *¼ cup (¾ oz./20 g) ground almonds*
- *1 egg yolk beaten with a few drops of water for glazing*

TO DECORATE
- *2¼ lb. (1 kg) beautiful fresh black figs (at least 8 large figs or 10 medium ones)*
- *Confectioners' sugar for dusting*

MAKE THE FIG COMPOTE

The day before, using an immersion blender, blend all the ingredients together. Cover and keep chilled.

MAKE THE PASTRY FOR THE TARTLET SHELLS

In the bowl of a stand mixer, beat the butter until creamy. Add, in the following order, the confectioners' sugar, the egg yolk, the flour and then the ground almonds, combining everything to make a smooth dough. Roll out the dough ⅛ in. (3 mm) thick. Using a cookie cutter, stamp out 8 disks, 4¾ in. (12 cm) in diameter, and line them into 8 pastry rings, 3 in. (8 cm) in diameter. Thoroughly prick the base of each pastry case with a fork and let rest for 1 hour in the refrigerator.

Preheat the oven to 325°F (160°C/Gas mark 3). Line each case with a disk of parchment paper and fill with ceramic baking beans or dried beans. Bake in the oven for 10 minutes. Remove the beans and the paper, brush the insides of the cases with the egg and water glaze and return to the oven for 1 minute. Do not switch off the oven, but raise its temperature to 450°F (230°C/Gas mark 8).

TO FINISH

Cut the fresh figs into even-sized cubes of at least ½ in. (1 cm). Generously fill the tartlet cases with the cubed figs (allow 1 large fig per tartlet), add the fig compote and slivered almonds. Return to the oven for 9 minutes.

Just before serving, dust the tartlets with confectioners' sugar.

GRATED
FENNEL

In the words of
FRANÇOIS PERRET

A pâtissier is a little bit like a *sculptor*, the more different materials he has at his disposal, the more he can experiment. And who said that a vegetable was a vegetable and an ingredient reserved for a cook? Too often we associate patisserie with the world of sugar, whereas the *realm of possibilities* stretches way beyond that. For example, it is not unusual for me to introduce a small vegetable element into my desserts. When I suggested *sweet-savory menus* for the Salon Proust, I wanted to go even further, to break through this boundary and head off in search of adventure: to show that a pâtissier could create an entire meal perfectly. An asparagus spear poached in sugar is delicious. Parmesan with hazelnut and meringue make the perfect match. And fennel goes beautifully with a *sweet vinaigrette*... For these menus, I work with sugar almost like I do with salt. It becomes the quintessential *seasoning* that allows the flavor of the ingredients to reveal themselves in all their *glory.*

Grated fennel

— *vinaigrette, and lemon sorbet* —

If you are short of time, you can buy the lemon sorbet from your artisan ice cream and sorbet maker.

SERVES 6

Prep: 1 hr. 30 min. (the fennel foam, lemon sorbet, and candied lemon need to be made the day before)
Cook: 1 hr. 10 min.

FENNEL FOAM

· 1¼ tsp. (3 g) fennel seeds
· ⅓ cup (75 ml) whole milk
· ⅓ cup (75 ml) whipping cream
· 2¾ cups (11½ oz./330 g) fromage blanc
· 5 tsp. (¾ oz./20 g) superfine sugar
· 3 sheets (6 g) gelatin

LEMON SORBET

· 1 cup (250 ml) water
· 3½ oz. (100 g) atomized glucose powder
· 2½ tbsp. (1 oz./30 g) superfine sugar
· 2 tsp. (10 g) powdered milk
· Finely grated zest of 1 lemon
· Scant ½ cup (100 ml) lemon juice

CANDIED LEMON

· 1 or 2 lemons (depending on size)
· *Syrup 1:* 1 cup (7 oz./200 g) superfine sugar and 1¾ cups (400 ml) water
· *Syrup 2:* ½ cup (3½ oz./100 g) superfine sugar and generous ¾ cup (200 ml) water

MAKE THE FENNEL FOAM

The day before, roast the fennel seeds for 10 minutes on a baking sheet in a 275°F (140°C/Gas mark 1) oven. Crush them in a pestle and mortar. Bring the milk and cream to a boil with the crushed seeds. Remove from the heat, cover with plastic wrap (cling film), let cool, and then leave overnight to infuse. The next day, strain through a fine-mesh sieve. Add the fromage blanc and the sugar. Soften the gelatin sheets in water, squeeze them out and melt in a bowl in a microwave. Stir into the cream mixture. Pour the mixture into a siphon fitted with a gas cartridge. Keep chilled.

MAKE THE LEMON SORBET

The day before, heat the water with the atomized glucose powder, sugar, powdered milk, and lemon zest to dissolve the powders. Bring to a boil, cover, let cool, and then add the lemon juice. Cover and allow to mature overnight in the refrigerator. The next day, churn in a sorbet maker. Store in the freezer.

MAKE THE CANDIED LEMON

The day before, cut the lemons into 4 or 6 wedges, depending on the size of the lemons. Remove the pith and most of the flesh, leaving a little of the flesh still attached to the peel. Blanch the peel three times in boiling water.

To make syrup 1, bring the sugar and water to a boil. Immerse the lemon peel in it, cover and let simmer gently for about 1 hour, without letting the temperature of the syrup rise above 158°F (70°C) on an instant-read thermometer. When the peel is tender, strain it.

To make syrup 2, combine the sugar and water and bring the temperature to 225°F (107°C) on an instant-read thermometer, pour it over the lemon peel and cover. Let cool and keep in the refrigerator in a sealed container.

FEUILLETINE SABLE PASTRY
- ¼ cup (2 oz./55 g) butter from Étrez, softened
- ¼ cup (1 oz./30 g) confectioners' sugar
- ⅓ cup (1 oz./30 g) ground almonds
- ½ cup (2 oz./55 g) all-purpose flour
- 1 oz. (25 g) feuilletine (or lacy crepes), crushed

FENNEL SUGAR TUILES
- 1 tbsp. (8 g) fennel seeds
- 8 oz. (225 g) fondant
- 5 oz. (150 g) glucose syrup

FENNEL WITH LEMON VINAIGRETTE
- 4 fennel bulbs
- Water and ice cubes
- 3½ tbsp. (50 ml) olive oil
- 4 tsp. (20 ml) kalamansi citrus vinegar (Huilerie beaujolaise®)
- 4 tsp. (20 ml) Pacific® (alcohol-free pastis)
- 2½ tbsp. (¾ oz./20 g) confectioners' sugar

FOR DRESSING THE PLATES
- Sprigs of wild fennel

MAKE THE FEUILLETINE SABLE PASTRY
Mix together the butter, confectioners' sugar, ground almonds, and flour. Add the crushed feuilletine and mix lightly to just combine the ingredients and make a smooth dough. Roll it out ¹⁄₁₆ in. (1.5 mm) thick between two sheets of parchment paper and chill it in the refrigerator (still between the sheets of parchment paper) until firm.

Preheat the oven to 350°F (180°C/Gas mark 4), ventilated setting. Slide the pastry onto a baking sheet, remove the top sheet of parchment paper, turn the pastry over onto a non stick baking sheet, and remove the other sheet of paper. Bake in the oven for 8 minutes.

MAKE THE FENNEL SUGAR TUILES
Crush the fennel seeds in a pestle and mortar. Preheat the oven to 350°F (180°C/Gas mark 4), not on ventilated setting.

In a saucepan, mix the fondant and glucose syrup together and then heat until the temperature reaches 329°F (165°C) on an instant-read thermometer. Pour the mixture onto a silicone baking mat and let cool. Process to a fine powder and then sift this powder onto a silicone baking mat through a small, fine-mesh sieve. Spread the powder over the mat to cover it in a thin sheet. Dust lightly and evenly with the crushed fennel seeds. Cook in the oven until completely melted. Remove the baking mat with the sugar sheet on it from the oven, let cool, then break the sheet into quite big pieces, and store them in a sealed container in a dry place.

MAKE THE VINAIGRETTE AND DRESS THE PLATES
Cut each fennel bulb into 4 pieces. Using a knife, remove the hearts and then shave them into fine ribbons using a truffle grater or a mandoline. Keep the shavings in a bowl of iced water. Meanwhile, make the vinaigrette by mixing the other ingredients together. Drain the fennel ribbons, pat them dry with paper towel and then dress them with the vinaigrette.

Place broken pieces of the feuilletine sable pastry in the center of each serving plate and top with a scoop of lemon sorbet. Cover completely with fennel foam from the siphon. Arrange the dressed fennel ribbons and drained candied lemon on each plate. Finally, add sprigs of wild fennel and a large broken piece of fennel sugar tuile to each.

Recipe photograph, following page.

Tart

— *with blackberries and celery* —

SERVES 8

Prep: 2 hr. 30 min.
(the celery bonbons and the sorbet need
to be made the day before)
Cook: 5 hr.

BASIC CELERY JUICE

· *2 heads of celery*
· *Superfine sugar*

MI-CUIT CELERY BONBONS

· *1 cup (250 ml) basic celery juice*
· *Generous 1⅓ cups (11 oz./310 g)*
  superfine sugar
· *½ head of celery*

CELERY SORBET

· *2¾ cups (650 ml) basic celery juice*
· *5 oz. (140 g) atomized glucose powder*
· *¾ tsp (4 g) SuperNeutrose® stabilizer*

PASTRY CREAM FOAM

· *2 sheets (4 g) gelatin*
· *10½ oz. (300 g) pastry cream*
  (see page 148)
· *¼ cup (1¾ oz./50 g) egg white*
  (about 2 medium whites)
· *Scant ½ cup (100 ml) crème*
  gastronomique from Étrez

MAKE THE BASIC CELERY JUICE

The day before, separate the celery stalks, wash and wipe them dry with paper towel. Put the celery through a juice extractor (without the leaves). Add sugar equivalent to 20% of the weight of the juice (being 1 cup/7 oz./200 g) sugar per 4 cups/1 liter of juice). Bring to a boil, skimming any impurities from the surface, and strain through a juice strainer with a filter bag. The juice must be very green.

MAKE THE MI-CUIT CELERY BONBONS

Prepare this the day before, just after you have extracted the juice from the celery. Add the sugar to the juice, heat it gently to dissolve the sugar and then let cool.
Cut the celery stalks into strips, ⅛–¼ in. (3–4) mm thick—no more. Place them in sous-vide bags, add the cold syrup, seal the bags sous-vide and leave to marinate in the refrigerator until the next day.

MAKE THE CELERY SORBET

The day before, bring the celery juice to a boil with the atomized glucose powder and then add the sugar and stabilizer. Churn in a sorbet maker and then spread out the made sorbet on a baking sheet, ¼ in. (5 mm) thick. Freeze and then, using a cookie cutter, stamp out 8 disks, 2½ in. (6 cm) in diameter. Keep in the freezer.

MAKE THE PASTRY CREAM FOAM

Soak the gelatin sheets until softened, squeeze them out, and melt in a bowl in a microwave. Add the dissolved gelatin to the other ingredients in a mixing bowl and process, using an immersion blender. Pour the mixture into a siphon fitted with a gas cartridge.

Recipe photograph, previous page.

BLACKBERRY CONSERVE

· 12 oz. (330 g) wild blackberries
· 2 tbsp. (30 ml) crème de mûre
  (blackberry liqueur)
· 2 tsp. (10 ml) gin
· ⅓ cup (3 oz./80 g) brown sugar mixed
  with ¾ tsp. (4 g) yellow pectin

PUFF PASTRY CRUST

· ⅓ cup (3 oz./80 g) fine brown sugar
· 1 lb. 2 oz. (500 g) puff pastry
  (see recipe on page 104)

MAKE THE BLACKBERRY CONSERVE

Halve the blackberries. Mix them with the crème de mûre, the gin, and the sugar and pectin mix. In saucepan, bring to a boil, lower the heat so the mixture is just simmering and cook for 5 minutes. Strain through a fine-mesh sieve and collect the juice, which will be used to glaze the blackberries. Chill the conserve in a tightly sealed plastic container.

MAKE THE PUFF PASTRY CRUST

Sift the brown sugar so it has as fine a texture as possible. Roll out the puff pastry, ⅛ in. (2.5 mm) thick, dust it with the fine brown sugar, and roll to a thickness of ¹⁄₁₆ in. (1.5 mm). Fold up and cut the pastry into strips, ¾ × 10¼ in. (2 × 26 cm). Place in the freezer to firm them up.

ASSEMBLE AND FINISH

Bake the puff pastry strips in a panini grill at 350°F (180°C) for about 15 seconds. As soon as you remove them from the grill, immediately roll them around a cookie cutter, 2¾ in. (7 cm) in diameter.
Using a small sieve, dust a little celery powder over each serving plate. Top with a puff pastry ring. Add a little pastry cream from the siphon in the center of each ring, taking care that the cream adheres to the pastry edges. Add a spoonful of blackberry conserve.

Place a scoop of celery sorbet in the center and then position the wild blackberries attractively and glaze with the juice collected from making the conserve. Decorate with drained celery bonbons.

Green asparagus
— *& genmaicha green tea* —

SERVES 8

Prep: 2 hr. (the asparagus foam is made the day before)
Cook: 15 min.

2 or 3 bunches of green asparagus

ASPARAGUS ICE CREAM

· *6 oz. (170 g) green asparagus, peeled*
· *Generous ¾ cup (200 ml) whole milk*
· *¼ cup (65 ml) crème gastronomique from Étrez*
· *3½ tbsp. (1½ oz./40 g) superfine sugar*
· *2 tsp. (10 g) powdered milk*
· *1 pinch (1 g) stabilizer Stab 2000*
· *Small pinch (0.5 g) fleur de sel*
· *Small pinch (0.5 g) Cambodian Kampot red pepper*

ASPARAGUS RIBBONS

· *2 peeled asparagus spears per person*
· *2 cups (500 ml) water*
· *½ cup (3½ oz./100 g) superfine sugar*

PREPARE THE ASPARAGUS

Select 2 perfect asparagus spears for each serving (16 in total). Using a sharp knife, cut off the woody ends of all the asparagus spears and also remove the small "scales" (reserve them for dressing the plates). Cut the 16 spears for garnish into 4 in. (10 cm) lengths. Keep the best pieces amongst the lengths that remain for the ribbons. Keep some of the asparagus that is left for the ice cream and, separately, the "scales" and pieces that are too thin to be sliced on a mandoline.

MAKE THE ASPARAGUS ICE CREAM

Slice the asparagus into rounds, reserving the tips. Cook the rounds in the milk and cream for 10 minutes at a gentle boil over low heat. Remove the saucepan from the heat, cover it with plastic wrap (cling film) and let infuse for 15 minutes. Add a little extra milk to make the quantity up to the original generous ¾ cup (200 ml). Process in a Thermomix until the texture is very smooth and then add the sugar, powdered milk, and stabilizer. Boil for 3 minutes, add the salt and pepper, taste, and adjust the seasoning as necessary. Keep the mixture in the freezer in Pacojet bowls.

MAKE THE ASPARAGUS RIBBONS

Using a truffle grater or a mandoline, shave the asparagus into ribbons. You will need 10 ribbons for each serving, 80 ribbons in total. Trim them so each is 3¾ in. (5 cm) long and put them in a plastic container. Bring the sugar and water to a boil to make a syrup and pour this over the ribbons. Cover with plastic wrap, pressing it over the surface of the ribbons in the syrup, and keep chilled.

ASPARAGUS FOAM

- ⅓ cup (75 ml) whole milk
- ⅓ cup (75 ml) whipping cream
- 1½ tsp. (7 g) genmaicha green tea (Japanese green tea with roasted brown rice)
- 3 sheets (6 g) gelatin
- 3⅓ cups (14½ oz./410 g) fromage blanc
- 5 tsp. (¾ oz./20 g) superfine sugar

TO DRESS THE PLATES

- 1 brioche (see recipe, page 28. or buy the brioche from your baker or pâtissier)
- 1 wedge of Parmesan Reggiano DOP
- 2 Meyer lemons (1 for segments, 1 for zest for dressing the plates)
- Extra virgin olive oil
- Brown sugar crystals

MAKE THE ASPARAGUS FOAM

The day before, bring the milk and cream to a boil, remove from the heat and add the genmaicha tea. Cover with plastic wrap and let infuse overnight. The next day, strain through a fine-mesh sieve, measure the liquid and add extra milk and cream (in equal quantities) to make up to the original quantity. Soak the gelatin to soften it, squeeze out the sheets, and melt in a bowl in a microwave. Add the fromage blanc and sugar, mixing well, and transfer to a siphon fitted with a gas cartridge. Keep chilled.

TO FINISH AND DRESS THE PLATES

Cut the brioche into 24 slices, $\frac{1}{16}$ in. (1.5 mm) thick, using a ham slicer. Place the slices in a yule log mold to make them curved and put them in a medium oven for a few minutes to toast them.

Using a cheese grater with large holes, grate the parmesan onto a non-stick baking sheet. Bake for a few minutes in a 350°F (180°C/Gas mark 4) oven until golden. Let cool. If you do this in advance, keep the parmesan "tuiles" in a dry place.

Peel one of the raw lemons. Remove the segments with a sharp knife and then cut each segment into 3 cubes.

Transfer the asparagus ice cream mixture to the Pacojet.

Wrap the asparagus ribbons into curls of 10 ribbons each and place one curl in the center of each serving plate in a circle, 3 in. (8 cm) in diameter. Place a cube of Meyer lemon in each circle, surround the asparagus with foam from the siphon (which must stay softer than for the honey dessert), add a few pieces of parmesan "tuile", and a thin stream of olive oil. Add 3 small quenelles of asparagus ice cream and decorate each with a thin strip of freshly cut Meyer lemon zest, and brioche toasts. Scatter over the reserved asparagus "scales". Finally, sprinkle over a few brown sugar crystals for extra flavor.

Recipe photographs, following pages.

Hazelnut meringue
— *aged parmesan, and lemon sauce* —

SERVES 8

*Prep: 1 hr. (make the fromage blanc
cream the day before)
Cook: 3 hr.*

FROMAGE BLANC CREAM
· *Scant ½ cup (3⅓ oz./100 g)
  fromage blanc from Étrez*
· *2½ tsp. (10 g) superfine sugar*
· *2 sheets (4 g) gelatin*
· *Scant ½ cup (100 ml) crème
  gastronomique from Étrez*

HAZELNUT MERINGUE
· *⅔ cup (5¼ oz./150 g) egg white
  (about 5 large whites)*
· *1 cup plus 1 tbsp. (8 oz./225 g)
  superfine sugar*
· *Coarsely chopped hazelnuts*

HAZELNUT PRALINE
· *⅓ cup (2¼ oz./66 g) superfine sugar*
· *Scant 1 cup (220 ml) water*
· *⅔ cup (3½ oz./100 g) white hazelnuts
  from Piedmont*
· *1 pinch (1 g) fleur de sel*

LEMON SAUCE
· *Generous ¾ cup (200 ml) water*
· *2½ tsp. (10 g) superfine sugar*
· *1½ tsp. (6 g) potato flour*
· *1½ tbsp. (25 ml) lemon juice*
· *½ tsp. (1.5 g) finely grated lemon zest*

FOR DRESSING THE PLATES
· *1 wedge of Parmesan Reggiano DOP*
· *1 or 2 unwaxed (organic) lemons,
  for the zest*
· *Chopped hazelnuts*

MAKE THE FROMAGE BLANC CREAM

The day before, using an immersion blender, blend together the fromage blanc and sugar. Soak the gelatin sheets in a little cold water until softened, squeeze them out and dissolve them in a microwave in a small bowl. Add the dissolved gelatin to the blended mixture. Whisk the *crème gastronomique* to soft peaks (do this carefully as it curdles easily; it must remain soft, so do not overbeat it). Using a flexible spatula, fold the two mixtures together. Spoon the cream into a pastry bag fitted with a no. 10 tip and keep it in the refrigerator until the next day.

MAKE THE HAZELNUT MERINGUE

Preheat the oven to 175°F (80°C/Gas on lowest setting). Whisk the egg whites until stiff, adding the sugar, a little at a time, and heating them gently with a blow torch. When the meringue is very stiff and shiny, spoon it into a pastry bag fitted with a sultan piping tip (a tip with a fluted ring and hollow center). Pipe it onto upturned flexible silicone molds for petits fours (*mignardises*) with flower-shaped cups, to make 48 meringues. Dust them with the chopped hazelnuts and bake the meringues for 3 hours in the oven. If, at the end of that time, the meringues are not yet dry, bake them for longer.

MAKE THE HAZELNUT PRALINE

In a saucepan, heat the sugar and water to 230°F (110°C) using an instant-read thermometer and then add the hazelnuts. Stir the nuts until the syrup crystallizes around them. Continue to stir until the hazelnuts are caramelized. Tip this mixture onto a baking sheet lined with parchment paper or a silicone baking mat and sprinkle over the salt. Leave to cool and then coarsely grind everything together—the praline must be granular, not ground too finely.

MAKE THE LEMON SAUCE

In a saucepan, mix all the ingredients together, except the lemon zest, and boil for 1 minute. Remove from the heat, add the lemon zest, let cool, and reserve.

DRESS THE PLATES

Grate the parmesan using a Microplane® grater. Fill the bottoms of the meringues with the fromage blanc cream, leaving a hollow for the hazelnut praline. Sandwich the meringues in pairs with the cream sides together. Arrange 3 meringues on each plate and fill the hollows with the hazelnut praline. Grate the parmesan generously over everything and then repeat by grating over the lemon zest. Add the chopped hazelnuts and serve the lemon sauce separately in a sauce boat.

GRAND
EVENING
DESSERTS

Rhubarb

SERVES 8

Prep: 2 hr., plus chilling time
Rest: 24 hr. (make the meringue
and the rhubarb juice, ribbons, and
mi-cuite bonbons the day before)

FRENCH MERINGUE
· *½ cup (3½ oz./100 g) egg whites*
· *½ cup (½ oz./100 g) superfine sugar*
· *⅓ cup (1½ oz./40 g) confectioners'*
  sugar, sifted

RHUBARB JUICE, RIBBONS,
AND MI-CUITE BONBONS
· *9 lb. (4 kg) rhubarb*
· *1½ cups (10½ oz./300 g) superfine*
  sugar

POACHED RHUBARB
· *1 cup (7 oz./200 g) superfine sugar*
· *4¼ cups (1 liter) water*
· *Grenadine syrup*
· *Reserved rhubarb*

GOAT CHEESE MOUSSE
· *⅓ cup (2¾ oz./80 g) fromage blanc*
· *Generous ⅓ cup (3 oz./90 g) fresh*
  goat cheese
· *2 sheets (4 g) gelatin*
· *Scant ½ cup (100 ml)*
  whipping cream

MAKE THE FRENCH MERINGUE

In a stand mixer, whisk the egg whites, gradually whisking in the superfine sugar to stiffen the whites. Switch off the mixer and fold in the confectioners' sugar with a flexible spatula. Spoon the meringue into a pastry bag with a plain tip and pipe droplets of meringue onto a silicone baking sheet. Flatten them with the back of a small, damp spoon. Put the meringues in an étuve and leave overnight.

MAKE THE RHUBARB JUICE, RIBBONS, AND MI-CUITE BONBONS

All three need to be prepared the day before. Start by making the rhubarb ribbons. Wash, lightly peel, and wipe the rhubarb. Cut 40 slices, ½ in. (1 cm) thick (5 per serving) and set aside. Keep the rest of the rhubarb for making the poached ribbons.
Collect all the trimmings and the remaining rhubarb and put them through a centrifugal juice extractor. Heat gently without boiling, skim, and then filter it through a strainer with a bag. It must be pink and translucent.
For the bonbons, measure 1 cup (250 ml) of rhubarb juice, boil it with the sugar and allow to cool completely. Mix the syrup with the rhubarb slices and put them in a sous-vide bag. Let marinate in the refrigerator.

MAKE THE POACHED RHUBARB

Make a syrup by bringing the sugar and water to a boil. Add sufficient grenadine syrup to color the syrup your desired shade. Slice the rest of the rhubarb into fine ribbons, $\frac{1}{16}$ in. (1.4 mm) thick, on a mandoline. Spread the ribbons out on a stainless steel tray, pour the boiling syrup over them, cover with plastic wrap (cling film), and allow to cool. Check the consistency of the rhubarb: it must be poached but still crisp. If it has not been poached enough, repeat the operation by collecting the syrup, bringing it to a boil, and pouring it once again over the rhubarb. Cover with plastic wrap and let cool.

MAKE THE GOAT CHEESE MOUSSE

Mix the fromage blanc and goat cheese together. Soak the gelatin in cold water to soften it, squeeze out excess water, melt the gelatin in a bowl in a microwave and mix it into the fromage blanc and goat cheese. Whip the cream and fold this in as well. Spoon the mousse into a pastry bag fitted with a smooth no. 6 tip and keep in the refrigerator.

RHUBARB SAUCE
· ¾ cup (190 ml) rhubarb juice
· ¼ cup (1 oz./30 g) confectioners' sugar
· ¼ tsp. (1.5 g) xanthan gum

RHUBARB SORBET
· 2¾ cups (650 ml) rhubarb juice
· 5 oz. (140 g) atomized glucose powder
· 2½ tbsp. (30 g) superfine sugar
· ¾ tsp. (4 g) Super-Neutrose stabilizer
· 2 tbsp. (30 ml) grenadine syrup

FOR DRESSING THE PLATES
· Sprigs of Lemon Basil Cress Koppert®

MAKE THE RHUBARB TUBES

Drain the thin rhubarb ribbons and spread them out over paper towel to dry them lightly. Pipe perfect logs of goat cheese mousse and roll the rhubarb ribbons around them to create tubes. Keep them in the freezer so you can slice them more easily later.

MAKE THE RHUBARB SAUCE

Blend the rhubarb juice with the confectioners' sugar and the xanthan gum. Keep chilled.

MAKE THE RHUBARB SORBET

Boil the rhubarb juice with the atomized glucose powder. Add the sugar and the stabilizer, bring back to a boil, and add the grenadine syrup. Cool and then churn. Store in the freezer.

DRESSING THE PLATES

Take the rhubarb-wrapped logs of mousse out of the freezer. For each serving, cut them into the following lengths:
1⅜ in. (3.5 cm)
2¾ in. (7 cm)
3⅓ in. (8.6 cm)
4 in. (10.3 cm)
5¾ in. (14.6 cm)
5⅓ in. (13.6 cm)
4¾ in. (12.2 cm)
3¾ in. (9.7 cm)
3¼ in. (8.1 cm)

Arrange them on the plates in the order given above. Brush the rhubarb sauce over the tubes. Position the meringue droplets and some small quenelles of sorbet on top. Decorate with sprigs of Lemon Basil Cress and mi-cuite rhubarb bonbons. Serve with the rhubarb sauce.

Recipe photographs, following pages.

Meyer lemon

The Meyer lemon is a citrus fruit originally from China that is now very popular in California. It was the result of crossing a lemon tree with a mandarin tree. It has a thin, soft skin, is yellow-orange in color, with a unique, very aromatic, fragrance and I love using it in my desserts. If the zest is too soft to be removed with a vegetable peeler, put the lemons in the freezer for half an hour before peeling them.

SERVES 8

Prep: 2 hr.
Rest: 1 hr. (plus 24 hr. for the puff pastry and 36 hr. for the meringue)
Cook: 20 min.

PUFF PASTRY
· *4¾ cups (15 oz./430 g) pastry flour (type T45)*
· *1½ cups (6½ oz./185 g) all-purpose flour*
· *Scant ½ cup (3⅓ oz./95 g) butter*
· *Scant 1¼ cups (270 ml) water*
· *1 tbsp. (15 g) Guérande salt*
· *Generous 2 cups (17½ oz./500 g) dry butter (beurre sec or beurre de tourage) with 84% butterfat*

LEMONS
· *16 Meyer lemons (have more in case you are short of juice)*

MEYER LEMON ZEST PASTE
· *1 cup (5 oz./150 g) finely grated Meyer lemon zest*
· *Scant 1 cup (220 ml) Meyer lemon juice*
· *Scant ½ cup (3 oz./80 g) superfine sugar*

LEMON SAUCE
· *½ tsp. (2 g) potato flour*
· *Generous ¾ cup (200 ml) juice saved from the previous step*

MAKE THE PUFF PASTRY
Sift the flours into the bowl of a stand mixer. Melt the butter. Stir the water and salt together and add them to the flours in the bowl with the melted butter. Mix until you have a smooth dough. Remove it from the bowl, shape it into a square, wrap in plastic wrap (cling film) and let rest in the refrigerator for 24 hours. Roll out the dough to a square and place the dry butter in the center. The butter must be half the size of the dough. Fold the dough over the butter and seal the edges so they are airtight. Give the dough five turns: for each turn, roll out the dough to a long rectangle, fold it into three and let it rest in the refrigerator for 1 hour. After the fifth turn, chill the dough again for 1 hour and then roll it out ⅛ in. (3 mm) thick and trim to 15 × 23½ in. (40 × 60 cm). Store in the refrigerator.

PREPARE THE LEMONS
Using a vegetable peeler, remove the zest from the lemons, peel away the pith, remove the segments with a sharp knife, and finally squeeze the remains of the lemons to extract the juice.

MAKE THE MEYER LEMON ZEST PASTE
Coarsely chop the lemon zest in a Thermomix. Add the Meyer lemon juice and superfine sugar, and let infuse for 1 hour. Blend again lightly. Strain through a fine-mesh sieve, pressing the zest to extract as much juice as possible. Reserve this juice, which will be used in the next step.
Blend the zest again in the Thermomix until it becomes a smooth paste. If it looks too dry, moisten it with about 4 tsp. (20 ml) of juice.

MAKE THE LEMON SAUCE
Mix the potato flour with a little of the reserved juice and then pour the rest of the juice into a saucepan. Bring to a boil, remove from the heat, let cool, and then chill.

LEMON MOUSSE
· 5 oz. (150 g) Mayer lemon zest paste
· 3 oz. (90 g) sweetened condensed milk
· 6 tbsp. (90 ml) crème gastronomique
   from Étrez
· ¾ cup (6 fl. oz./180 ml) whipping cream

PUFF PASTRY PALMIERS
· Sheets of puff pastry (see opposite)
· Superfine sugar

MERINGUE
· ½ cup (4 oz./110 g) egg whites
· 1 cup (6 oz./170 g) superfine sugar

TO SERVE
· Crème gastronomique from Étrez

MAKE THE LEMON MOUSSE

Using a flexible spatula, mix the lemon zest paste, the condensed milk, and the *crème gastronomique* together. Lightly whip the cream (it must be mousse-like but not too stiff) and fold it into the lemon paste mixture, again using a flexible spatula. Spoon this mixture into a pastry bag.

MAKE THE PUFF PASTRY PALMIERS

Divide the rolled-out puff pastry lengthwise into three equal pieces. Roll out each piece ¹⁄₁₆ in. (1 mm) thick. Stack them on top of each other, dusting ½ cup (3½ oz./100 g) sugar between the three layers. Roll out again so the total thickness of the pastry layers is ¼ in. (4.5 mm) and then chill the pastry in the freezer until firm. Cut into strips 8½ in. (22 cm) long and stick them together in threes, side by side, to give them a wavy shape as in the photograph. You can use tubes to produce the wavy effect, but you can also leave them flat. Repeat with the remaining puff pastry.
Preheat the oven to 400°F (200°C/Gas mark 6). Place the puff pastry palmiers on a non-stick baking sheet and bake them in the oven for about 20 minutes.

MAKE THE MERINGUE

In a stand mixer, whisk the egg whites with the sugar. When the meringue is standing in soft peaks, place the bowl of the mixer in a bain-marie until the temperature reaches 122°F (50°C), continuing to whisk the whites until they are firm. Using a droplet-shaped cardboard template, pipe the meringue onto a silicone baking mat. Carefully lift the meringue droplets into a stainless steel yule log mold so they are slightly curved. Dry them in an étuve for 36 hours.

TO DRESS THE PLATES

Place two puff pastry palmiers upright on their side on each plate, facing each other. Pipe the lemon mousse one-third of the way up the palmiers so they stand up.
Arrange Meyer lemon segments in different directions on top, creating volume. Place four meringue droplets on the lemon segments on each plate. Pour a little *crème gastronomique* from Étrez on each meringue and then finish by adding the lemon sauce.

Recipe photograph, following page.

Wild blueberry crackers

*The cracker pastry recipe is inspired by Michel Troisgros,
to whom I am indebted for this plated dessert.*

SERVES 10

Prep: 2 hr.
Rest and dry: 5 hr. 30 min.
Cook: 3 hr. 45 min.

CRACKER DOUGH
· *2¾ cups (9 oz./250 g) pastry flour*
  (type T45)
· *2¼ tbsp. (35 ml) olive oil*
· *1 oz. (30 g) organic baker's yeast*
· *Scant ½ cup (100 ml) warm water*
· *2 tsp. (10 g) fleur de sel*

BLUEBERRY JUICE
· *1 lb. 2 oz. (500 g) wild blueberries*
· *¼ cup (1¾ oz./50 g) superfine sugar*

BLUEBERRY POWDER
· *3½ oz. (110 g) blueberries, reserved*
  from preparing the juice
· *2 tsp (8 g) superfine sugar*
· *1 tbsp (½ oz./15 g) egg white*
  (½ large white)

BLUEBERRY CONSERVE
· *Remaining blueberries, reserved*
  from preparing the juice
· *Superfine sugar, equal to 40% of*
  the weight of the blueberries

MAKE THE CRACKER DOUGH

Work the flour and olive oil together until the mixture has an even sandy texture. Crumble the yeast into the warm water, add the flour and then the salt. In the bowl of a stand mixer, beat at medium speed for 20 minutes. Transfer the dough to a bowl, cover it with plastic wrap (cling film) and leave to prove at room temperature for 30 minutes.
Preheat the oven to 425°F (220°C/Gas mark 7). Knead the dough very briefly, shape it into a long rectangle and fold it in three (first one third to the center and then the other). Roll it out ⅓ in. (8 mm) thick using a rolling machine or rolling pin. Cut the dough into 3-in. (8-cm) squares. Put them on a baking sheet and, as soon as they go in the oven, lower the temperature to 325°F (170°C/Gas mark 3). Bake for 6 minutes, turn the squares over and finish baking for 4 or 5 minutes. Do not let them color too much.

MAKE THE BLUEBERRY JUICE

Heat the ingredients in a bain-marie, over gentle heat, for 1 hour. Strain through a fine-mesh sieve, collecting the juice and reserving the fruit for the powder and conserve.

MAKE THE BLUEBERRY POWDER

Mix all the ingredients together and then roll out as thinly as possible on a silicone baking mat. Dry for 4 hours in a 160°F (70°C/Gas on lowest setting) oven and then blend to a powder. Keep dry in a sealed airtight container.

MAKE THE BLUEBERRY CONSERVE

Weigh the blueberries and add 40% of their weight in sugar. Put both in a saucepan, bring to a boil and then lower the heat and let simmer until the mixture is the desired thickness (do not blend).

Recipe photograph, previous page.

CLAFOUTIS ICE CREAM
· *Generous ¾ cup (200 ml) whole milk*
· *½ Bourbon vanilla bean*
· *⅓ cup (3 oz./80 g) egg yolk (4 large yolks)*
· *2 tbsp. (1 oz./30 g) brown sugar*
· *Scant ½ cup (100 ml) UHT cream*

MERINGUE
· *¼ cup (2 oz./60 g) egg white*
  (2 large whites)
· *⅓ cup (2 oz./60 g) superfine sugar*
· *½ cup (2 oz./60 g) confectioners' sugar,*
  sifted

SWEET SHORTCRUST PASTRY
· *⅔ cup (5 oz./150 g) butter, softened,*
  plus a little for the ring
· *⅔ cup (3 oz./90 g) confectioners' sugar*
· *1 oz. (30 g) ground almonds*
· *1 egg*
· *1 pinch (1 g) fleur de sel*
· *½ vanilla bean (only the seeds)*
· *2 cups (9 oz./250 g) all-purpose flour*

BLUEBERRY MIXTURE
· *10½ oz. (300 g) fresh blueberries*
· *3 oz. (90 g) blueberry conserve*

ÉTREZ CREAM SAUCE
· *1 cup (250 ml)*
  crème gastronomique from Étrez
· *1 tbsp. (12.5 ml) whipping cream*

MAKE THE CLAFOUTIS ICE CREAM
Bring the milk and vanilla bean, split lengthwise and seeds scraped out, to a boil. Remove from the heat. Whisk the egg yolks and brown sugar together to the ribbon stage. Add the hot milk, a little at a time, whisking constantly, and then cook over low-medium heat, stirring until the mixture thickens. Strain this cream through a fine-mesh sieve onto the UHT cream. Process with an immersion blender and then cook for about 40–45 minutes in a 250°F (130°C/Gas mark ½) oven, ventilated setting. The cream must be firm in the center. Let cool, put in a blast chiller (or freezer) until the mixture hardens and then blend until smooth. Transfer to Pacojet bowls as it is not suitable for churning in an ice cream machine.

MAKE THE MERINGUE
Whisk the egg whites in a stand mixer with the superfine sugar and then fold in the confectioners' sugar using a flexible spatula. Spoon the meringue into a pastry bag fitted with a plain no. 8 tip. Pipe logs of meringue onto a silicone baking mat the length of the mat. Bake them in a 190°F (90°C/Gas on lowest setting) oven for 1 hour.

MAKE THE SWEET SHORTCRUST PASTRY
Mix the softened butter with the confectioners' sugar and the ground almonds. Add the egg, fleur de sel, and vanilla seeds. Sift the flour and then gently incorporate it into the other ingredients until you have a smooth dough. Shape the dough into a ball, wrap it in plastic wrap and let rest in the refrigerator for 1 hour.
Preheat the oven to 325°F (160°C/Gas mark 3). Roll out the pastry ⅛ in. (2 mm) thick, place on a baking sheet and bake in the oven for 20 minutes. Let cool and then break the pastry into pieces.

ASSEMBLY
Process the ice cream mixture in a Pacojet and then transfer it to a pastry bag. Combine the fresh blueberries with the conserve to make the blueberry mixture.
Mix the two creams together to make the sauce.
Make a hole in the base of each cracker and fill it with the ice cream in the pastry bag. Add the blueberry mixture as well and finish with pieces of meringue and a little more ice cream. Fill generously but take care not to add too much ice cream or too much conserve. Block up the cracker holes with pieces of sweet shortcrust pastry to stop the crackers sliding on the plates.
Place a cracker in the middle of each plate and then coat with the cream sauce in front of your guests. Finish by dusting with the blueberry powder, sifted through a small sieve.

Wild blackberries

— *with meringue and whipped cream* —

SERVES 8
Prep: 1 hr.
Cook: 2 hr. 15 min.

MERINGUE SOUFFLÉ
· ⅔ cup (5¼ oz./150 g) fresh egg whites
· Scant 1 cup (5½ oz./160 g) superfine sugar
· ½ cup (2½ oz./70 g) confectioners' sugar,
  sifted

WHIPPED CREAM
· 4¼ cups (1 liter) whipping cream
· Generous ¾ cup (200 ml)
  crème gastronomique from Étrez

BLACKBERRY JUICE
· 2¼ lb. (1 kg) wild blackberries
· 3½ tbsp. (50 ml) crème de mûre
  (blackberry liqueur)
· 4 tsp. (20 ml) gin

BLACKBERRY COULIS
· ¾ tsp. (3 g) potato flour
· ⅓ cup (225 ml) blackberry juice

TO SERVE
· Confectioners' sugar
· Thick crème fraîche

MAKE THE MERINGUE SOUFFLÉ
Preheat the oven to 250°F (125°C/Gas mark ½), ventilated setting.
Whisk the whites in a stand mixer, adding the superfine sugar gradually,
and whisking until they stand in firm peaks. Switch off the mixer and fold
in the confectioners' sugar with a flexible spatula. Spoon the meringue
into a pastry bag and pipe it onto a silicone baking mat on the template as
shown (the disks are 1¾ in./4.5 cm in diameter). Make 8 shapes and bake
them for 1 hour 30 minutes in the oven.

PREPARE THE WHIPPED CREAM
Whip the two creams together without letting them become too stiff.
Spoon into a pastry bag fitted with a sultan tip (a large tip with a fluted
edge and hollow center for piping fluted rings) and keep in the refrigerator.

MAKE THE BLACKBERRY JUICE
Put all the ingredients in a bowl in a bain-marie and cook for 45 minutes
at 190°F (90°C), covering the bowl with plastic wrap (cling film). Allow
to cool and then strain through a jelly strainer with a bag. Reserve the
blackberries for making a conserve.

MAKE THE BLACKBERRY COULIS
Stir the potato flour into a little of the blackberry juice until smooth and
then add this mixture to the rest of the juice in a saucepan. Bring to a short
boil, cool, and keep in the refrigerator.

TO SERVE
Spoon the thick (heavy) cream into a pastry bag without a tip.
Place the meringues in the center of oval serving plates and then fill the
holes with the cream, taking care not to overfill them. Decorate generously with wild blackberries.
Take the pastry bag of whipped cream with the sultan tip and on each
meringue rosette pipe an identical rosette. Again, decorate generously
with wild blackberries.
Dust with confectioners' sugar and then place a spoonful of blackberry
coulis on each rosette.

MY SWEETEST MOMENTS

In three stages

The dessert menu at La Table de L'Espadon is called "The *Reward*," a description I consider wholly apt. Who has never been told "if you don't behave, you will not have dessert," while nobody ever threatens to deprive you of a meat pie! It just shows the importance attached to the latter. Dessert is a *bonus, the cherry on the cake*, the extra *pleasure*, the good bit you madly desire. It is rooted in our DNA. A "crazy thing" that follows us all our lives turning up at every *happy event*: baptisms, birthdays, holidays, achievements, marriages, reunions… It is also the *finale* to a meal that lingers in the mouth. It must be the perfect denouement, the *ultimate and deliciously sinful* pleasure. At La Table de L'Espadon with Chef Nicolas Sale, we wanted this "Reward" to be even more *spectacular and to arrive in three separate stages*, the Light Touch, the Dessert, and the Friandise (small sweet treat). Three interpretations of the same ingredient—caramel here—that would explore and *surprise* every *emotion*. I love this idea of one reward hiding another, and then another. To succeed in creating the *euphoria* of a winning trio which guests dining at La Table de L'Espadon will remember with *joy*.

Crème caramel

When someone creates a dessert, their primary objective is to bring together as many people as possible and please the greatest number they can. However, crème caramel is a dessert that already brings lots of people together… This idea has been the trigger for revisiting crème caramel to give it more depth, while still keeping its richness and bounteousness.

Caramel and milk mousse

SERVES 8

Prep: 20 min.

CARAMEL

- *1 cup (7 oz./200 g) superfine sugar*
- *Scant 1 cup (7 oz./200 g) butter, at room temperature, diced*
- *2½ tbsp. (35 ml) cold water*

MILK MOUSSE AND TO DRESS THE PLATES

- *1¾ cups (400 ml) whole milk from Étrez*
- *Fleur de sel*

MAKE THE CARAMEL

In a saucepan, heat the sugar until it melts and cooks to a caramel and then lower the temperature of the caramel by gradually adding the diced butter. Finally, add the cold water. If the mixture is not smooth, process it with an immersion blender. Keep chilled in a plastic container.

MAKE THE MILK MOUSSE

Bring the milk to a boil, take it off the heat, and using an immersion blender, process to make a milk mousse. Stop to let the milk deflate a few times so you can only lift off the firm mousse, without the liquid. Spoon the mousse into a disposable pastry bag and snip off the point.

TO DRESS THE PLATES

Spoon the caramel into a disposable pastry bag and snip off the point. Pipe the milk mousse into small dishes and then pipe a spiral of caramel over it. Finally, decorate with a few grains of fleur de sel.

The light touch

The dessert

Meringue with crisp, golden almonds

SERVES 8
Prep: 2 hr. Infuse the milk for the vanilla ice cream the day before.
Cook: 32 min.

VANILLA ICE CREAM
· 5 Bourbon vanilla beans
· 1¾ cups (420 ml) whole milk
· ¾ oz. (20 g) invert sugar
· ¾ cup (165 ml) thick crème fraîche
· ⅓ cup (3½ oz./100 g) egg yolk (about 5 large yolks)
· 2¼ tbsp. (35 g) powdered milk
· 3½ oz. (100 g) atomized glucose powder
· ½ cup (3½ oz./100 g) egg white (about 3 large whites)

CRISP, GOLDEN ALMONDS
· Scant ½ cup (100 ml) water
· ⅔ cup (4½ oz./130 g) superfine sugar
· ½ cup (3½ oz./100 g) slivered almonds

MERINGUE
· ⅔ cup (5¼ oz./150 g) fresh egg white (5 large whites)
· ¾ cup (5½ oz./160 g) superfine sugar
· ½ cup (2½ oz./70 g) confectioners' sugar, sifted

DRY CARAMEL
· 2½ cups (17½ oz./500 g) sugar
· 3½ tbsp. (50 ml) hot water

CRÈME CARAMEL
· 8 large whole eggs, plus 4 yolks
· ½ cup (3½ oz./100 g) superfine sugar
· 3¾ cups (1.6 liters) whole milk

CARAMEL FOR THE FLOATING ISLAND
· 1⅓ cups (9 oz./250 g) superfine sugar
· Scant ½ cup (100 ml) hot water

MAKE THE VANILLA ICE CREAM
The day before, split the vanilla beans lengthwise and scrape out the seeds. Bring the milk to a boil with the invert sugar, crème fraiche, vanilla beans, and seeds. Cover, let cool and then chill overnight in the refrigerator.
The next day, whisk the egg yolks. Bring the infused milk to a boil again, adding the powdered milk and atomized glucose powder. Pour a little of this still warm mixture onto the egg yolks, stirring constantly. Add the rest of the hot milk mixture and cook, stirring constantly as for a crème anglaise, until the temperature reaches 180°F (82°C) (the cream must coat the spatula). Strain through a fine-mesh sieve and cool completely before incorporating the egg whites. Churn and then store the ice cream in the freezer.

MAKE THE CRISP, GOLDEN ALMONDS
Preheat the oven to 350°F (180°C/ Gas mark 4). Heat the water and sugar to 86°F (30°C) to make a syrup. Using tweezers, dip the best-looking slivered almonds in the syrup, put them on a silicone baking mat and place in the oven for only 5–10 minutes, until the almonds are a good color.

MAKE THE MERINGUE
In a stand mixer, whisk the egg whites, gradually adding the sugar: the whites must be firm but not grainy. Switch off the mixer and fold in the confectioners' sugar with a flexible spatula. Spoon the meringue into a pastry bag fitted with a sultan tip (a large tip with a fluted edge and a hollow center for piping fluted rings) and pipe 40 straight logs, 1¼–1½ in. (3–4 cm) in diameter, without any bulge at the base. Keep in the freezer.

MAKE THE DRY CARAMEL
Cook the sugar over moderate heat until it melts and you have a deep brown caramel that is smoking lightly. Lower the temperature of the caramel with the hot

water and divide between 8 heatproof molds, 4¾ in. (12 cm) in diameter and ¾ in. (2 cm) deep.

MAKE THE CRÈME CARAMEL
Preheat the oven to 190°F (90°C/Gas on its lowest setting). Heat a saucepan of water until simmering and have a large ovenproof plate with a tall rim or a baking dish close to the stove.
Whisk the whole eggs, egg yolks, and sugar until pale and thick. Bring 3⅓ cups (800 ml) milk to a boil and pour it onto the egg mixture, whisking constantly. Add the rest of the cold milk. Pour into the molds over the caramel, allowing a generous ¾ cup (200 ml) for each mold. Pour the simmering water into the plate or baking dish. Cover the molds with plastic wrap (cling film) and stand them in the plate or dish. Cook for 22 minutes in the oven. Remove the plastic wrap and take the molds out of the oven.

MAKE THE CARAMEL FOR THE FLOATING ISLAND
Cook the sugar until it melts and you have a deep brown caramel. Lower the temperature of the caramel with the hot water, cool and chill.

ASSEMBLY
Before assembling, fill the meringues by piping in the vanilla ice cream. Keep in the freezer.
Unmold the crème caramels by running the blade of a knife around the inside of each mold. As you rotate the mold, release the crèmes caramels from the sides of the molds, taking care not to go back over an area already released. Pour out the excess caramel before unmolding. Center each crème caramel on a serving plate and then unmold. Place 5 filled meringues around each crème caramel and then add 5 golden almonds for each meringue. Fill the top of the meringues with the caramel for the floating island.

Cigarette russe

SERVES 8

Prep: 20 min.
Rest: 1 hr.
Cook: 5 min.

· 1 ⅔ cups (7 oz./200 g) all-purpose flour
· ⅔ cup (5 oz./145 g) butter, softened
· 1½ cups (7 oz./200 g)
  confectioners' sugar
· ¾ tsp (4 g) salt
· Scant 1 cup (7 oz./200 g) egg white
(about 7 large whites)

Sift the flour. Beat the butter until light. Beat in the confectioners' sugar and salt and then the sifted flour. Lastly add the egg whites and mix to make a batter. Let the batter rest in the refrigerator for at least 1 hour before baking.

Preheat the oven to 400°F (200°C/Gas mark 6), ventilated setting (for those in a professional kitchen: oura (air duct) open, ventilation setting 4).

Spread the batter, not too thinly, over a non-stick baking sheet. Mark it into 8 rectangles, measuring 2.5 × 6 in. (6 × 15 cm), either by hand or using a stencil. Bake for 5 minutes until a rich golden color. As soon as you remove the batter from the oven, roll each rectangle, still hot, around a tube, ¾ in. (1.5 cm) in diameter. It is very important to turn the rectangles over before you roll them.

Let cool before removing the cigarettes from the tube.

Something sweet

Strawberry

I like to steep strawberries in cream with sugar. In a punnet you find some excellent strawberries, some lovely surprises and… some disappointments. I therefore wanted to ensure the success of every strawberry, making it excellent, coating and glazing it and, at the same time, adding cream and sugar, which go so well.

Conserve, burrata, olive oil, and vinegar

SERVES 8

Prep: 10 min.

- *Strawberry vinegar or young balsamic vinegar*
- *2 balls of creamy burrata*
- *Extra virgin olive oil*
- *The remaining strawberry conserve from the strawberry dessert (see the following recipe)*
- *Fleur de sel*
- *Freshly ground Tasmanian pepper*

Use only the creamy hearts of the burrata.

For the strawberry conserve, see the following recipe. You will be using the leftover conserve.

Put into a bowl 6 drops of strawberry vinegar or, alternatively, balsamic vinegar but use quite a young one to avoid excess sugar. Add 2 small spoonfuls of burrata, 4 drops of olive oil, 3 strawberries or pieces of strawberry from the conserve, a little liquid from the conserve, and finally a little fleur de sel and freshly ground Tasmanian pepper.

The light touch

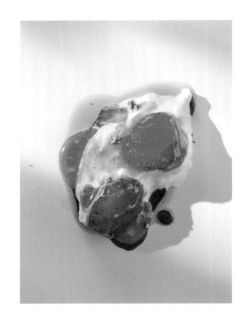

The dessert

Iced parfait enclosed in curls, pepper, and salt

SERVES 8
Prep: 2 hr.
Freeze: 2 hr.
Infuse: 24 hr., for the whipped cream
Cook: 2 min.

CHOCOLATE CIGARETTE BATTER CURLS
· ⅔ cup (3 oz./88 g) all-purpose flour
· Scant 2 tbsp. (13 g) unsweetened cocoa powder
· 7 tbsp. (3½ oz./100 g) best-quality unsalted butter, softened
· ¾ cup (3½ oz./100 g) confectioners' sugar
· Scant ½ cup (3¾ oz./105 g) egg white (about 3½ large whites)

ICED COCOA BEAN SOUFFLÉ
Mixture 1: *Sabayon*
· 1½ tbsp. (1½ oz./40 g) egg yolk (about 2 large yolks)
· 2 tbsp. (1 oz./25 g) brown sugar
· 4 tsp. (20 ml) water

Mixture 2: *Italian meringue*
· Generous ¼ cup (generous 2 oz./60 g) brown sugar
· 4 tsp. (20 ml) water
· 2 tbsp. (1 oz./30 g) egg white (about 1 large white)

Mixture 3: *Whipped cocoa cream*
· ¾ cup (180 ml) whipping cream
· 2 oz. (60 g) cocoa beans, ground
· ½ oz. (14 g) cacao nibs, chopped, to finish

CACAO NIBS SEASONING MIX
· 1¾ oz. (50 g) cacao nibs
· 1 pinch of Cambodian Kampot red pepper
· 1 tsp. (5 g) fleur de sel

CHOCOLATE JAMAYA GANACHE
· 2 oz. (60 g) chocolate Jamaya
· ⅔ cup (150 ml) crème gastronomique from Étrez

MAKE THE CHOCOLATE CURLS
Preheat the oven to 475°F (250°C / Gas at highest setting). Sift the flour with the cocoa powder. Beat the butter and confectioners' sugar together until light and creamy. Add the egg whites and then the sifted flour and cocoa, and mix to make a batter. Spread the batter thinly in the center of a silicone or non-stick baking sheet to a rectangle measuring 18 in. (45 cm) long × 2 in. (5 cm) wide. Using a chocolate comb, score lines through the batter, taking care to leave ⅓ in. (1 cm) of batter unscored. Bake in the oven for 2 minutes and do not move away, stay by the oven while the batter is cooking. As soon as you take the batter out of the oven, immediately roll it diagonally around a copper tube, 1⅓ in. (3.3 cm) in diameter. Let cool. In order to obtain 8 curls of cigarette batter, 5½–6 in. (14–15 cm) long, prepare three rolls, either repeating the process three times or using 3 baking sheets and 3 tubes.

MAKE THE ICED COCOA BEAN SOUFFLÉ
If you use a stand mixer to make the iced soufflé, I recommend that you double the quantities of ingredients to make the job easier. Begin by preparing the three mixtures and then combine them. Sabayon: lightly beat the egg yolks. Dissolve the brown sugar in the water and heat until the temperature reaches 240°F (115°C) on an instant-read thermometer. Pour the syrup onto the egg yolks, whisking continuously until combined. Italian meringue: heat the sugar and water until the temperature reaches 245°F (118°C) on a thermometer. Meanwhile, whisk the egg whites to firm peaks. Pour the hot syrup onto the egg whites in a thin, steady stream, whisking all the time. Continue whisking until the meringue is cold. Whipped cocoa cream: the day before,

mix the cream with the cocoa beans and leave in the refrigerator for 24 hours to infuse. The next day, strain through a fine-mesh sieve and add more cream to make the quantity up to the original ¾ cup (180 ml). Keep chilled. When ready to assemble the soufflé, whip the infused cream until thick.
First whisk the sabayon (1) with the Italian meringue (2) and then incorporate the whipped cocoa cream (3). Lastly add the chopped cacao nibs.
Spoon the mixture into three clear acetate tubes, 1¼ in. (3 cm) in diameter and 15¾ in. (40 cm) long. Freeze until hard and then divide into 8 sausages, 5 in. (13 cm) long. Return to the freezer.

MAKE THE CACAO NIBS SEASONING MIX
Blend all the ingredients together in a Thermomix to make quite a coarse powder.

MAKE THE CHOCOLATE JAMAYA GANACHE
Chop the chocolate and put it in a large bowl. Bring the cream to a boil and pour it in two, or even three, equal amounts onto the chocolate, stirring with a spatula until the cream and chocolate are evenly combined. This ganache must be used straight away.

ASSEMBLY
Before serving, warm plates and cloches in the oven or a steamer at 195°F (90°C). They must be very hot. Make the chocolate Jamaya ganache at the last moment. With the help of a small spatula, very carefully place the iced soufflés inside the cigarette batter curls. Position each in the center of a serving plate.
Spoon 3 pools of ganache around each dessert and, using a small strainer, dust over the seasoning mix. Serve immediately.

Recipe photograph, page 123.

Raspberries

SERVES 8
Prep: 40 min.
Cook: 7 min.

BLANCMANGE
- *⅓ cup (2½ oz./75 g) egg white (about 2½ large egg whites)*
- *⅓ cup (2 oz./60 g) superfine sugar*
- *1 sheet (2 g) gelatin*

JAMAYA CHOCOLATE NIBS
- *7 oz. (200 g) Jamaya chocolate*

RASPBERRY VINEGAR CONSERVE
- *1 lb. 2 oz. (500 g) frozen raspberries*
- *1⅓ cups (10½ oz./300 g) brown sugar*
- *4 tsp. (20 ml) lemon juice*
- *2 tsp. (10 ml) raspberry vinegar*

MAKE THE BLANCMANGE

In a stand mixer, whisk the egg whites with the sugar until they stiffen. Soak the gelatin, squeeze out the excess water and then melt in a microwave (only do this when the egg whites have been whisked). Add the hot, melted gelatin, mix and switch off the stand mixer. Spread out the blancmange mixture on a baking sheet in an even layer, ⅔ in. (1.5 cm) deep, and cook for 3 minutes in a steam oven at 176°F (80°C) (or in a steamer until it is just firm). Let cool and then, using a round cookie cutter, ¾ in. (2 cm) in diameter, cut out cylinders.

MAKE THE JAMAYA CHOCOLATE NIBS

Process the chocolate in a Thermomix and then sieve it to collect the chocolate nibs without the powder. Be careful not to blend the chocolate too much as you do not want to turn it into a fine powder, but granules that resemble coarse sand.

MAKE THE RASPBERRY VINEGAR CONSERVE

Bring the raspberries to a boil with the sugar. Add the lemon juice and cook for a few moments. Blend, pour into a saucepan and bring to a boil over a high heat. Cook for 3 minutes, stirring constantly. Pour into conserve pots and keep chilled.

For this recipe, use 2 oz. (60 g) of the preserve and sieve it to remove all the seeds. Add the raspberry vinegar. Spoon into a pastry bag fitted with a fine, plain tip.

TO FINISH

Roll the blancmange cylinders in the ground chocolate nibs. Place a small scoop of raspberry vinegar conserve on top of each in the center.

Something sweet

Honey

Honey is one of my fetish ingredients. Naturally pleasing and always good, for me it is the caviar of patisserie. Not only is it the finest quality sugar, it also adds flavor. It is a magic ingredient. In this sequence of recipes, I wanted it pure, to showcase it in all its brilliance, delicacy and power, to ensure it takes its rightful place. But if it is vital for a dessert to live up to its promise, one with honey in this instance, it is just as important that it does not reveal everything in the first mouthful! It must continue to surprise throughout, to be a seducer so you succumb more completely: to let you see, to dream, but without baring all from the beginning. Teasing people's desire could almost be my patisserie mantra.

Faisselle, honeyed red onion jam

SERVES 8
Prep: 30 min.
Cook: 4 hr.

HONEYED RED ONION JAM
· *2 red onions*
· *Grape seed oil*
· *Chestnut honey*

MERINGUE SOUFFLÉ
· *⅓ cup (2½ oz./75 g) egg white (about 2½ large whites)*
· *½ cup (3½ oz./110 g) superfine sugar*

TO DRESS THE PLATES
· *1 large tub of fromage blanc from Étrez*
· *Freeze-dried Tasmanian peppercorns*

MAKE THE HONEYED RED ONION JAM
Peel the onions and cut them into ¼-in. (5 mm) slices. Heat a little oil in a skillet. When it is hot, add the onion slices and sweat them for a few minutes without letting them color. Lower the heat, add 2 tablespoons of chestnut honey and cook over a low heat until the onions are candied (about 1 hour). Cool a little and then weigh. For 1 oz. (30 g) onion jam, add 2 tbsp. (40 g) chestnut honey. Let cool completely and then transfer to a pastry bag and store in the refrigerator.

MAKE THE MERINGUE SOUFFLÉ
Whisk the egg whites to make a meringue, adding the sugar a little at a time. Spoon the meringue into a pastry bag fitted with a plain tip. Pipe balls of meringue on a baking sheet lined with parchment paper and cook them in a 225°F (110°C/ Gas mark ¼) oven, ventilated setting, for 3 hours.

TO DRESS THE PLATES
Drain the fromage blanc from Étrez. Place a spoonful in shallow serving dishes. Pipe the onion jam on the fromage blanc. Break up the meringues and add them. Crush the Tasmanian peppercorns and dust them over each dessert, judging the amount you add carefully.

The light touch

The dessert

Honeycomb

SERVES 8

Prep: 2 hr.
Rest: 12 hr. (make the honey ice cream mixture the day before), plus 1 hour for the pastry
Cook: 25 min.

CIGARETTE BATTER
· *1 ⅔ cups (7 oz./200 g) all-purpose flour*
· *⅔ cup (5 oz./145 g) butter, softened*
· *1½ cups (7 oz./200 g) confectioners' sugar*
· *¾ tsp. (4 g) salt*
· *1 cup (7 oz./200 g) egg white*
  (about 7 large whites)

HONEY ICE CREAM
· *1¼ cups (300 ml) whole milk*
· *3½ tbsp. (50 ml) UHT whipping cream*
· *3 egg yolks*
· *2 tbsp. (1½ oz./ 40 g) acacia honey*
· *1 tbsp. (20 g) chestnut honey*
· *¾ oz. (20 g) powdered milk*
· *2½ tbsp. (40 ml) crème gastronomique*
  from Étrez

MILK FOAM
· *3 sheets (6 g) gelatin*
· *5 tbsp. (75 ml) whipping cream from Étrez*
· *5 tbsp. (75 ml) milk*
· *1½ tsp. (5 g) finely grated lemon zest*
· *1¼ tbsp. (15 g) superfine sugar*
· *14½ oz. (410 g) strained cottage cheese*

SANDED ALMONDS
· *1 cup (7 oz./200 g) whole blanched almonds*
· *⅔ cup (150 ml) water*
· *⅓ cup (2½ oz./75 g) superfine sugar*
· *¾ tsp. (4 g) fleur de sel*
· *1 tsp. (4 g) toasted almond oil*

PEAR SYRUP
· *4 pears (allow ½ per person)*
· *2 cups (500 ml) water*
· *½ cup (3½ oz./100 g) sugar*
· *2½ tbsp. (40 ml) pear eau-de-vie*
· *1½ tsp. (5 g) ascorbic acid*

TO DRESS THE PLATES
· *Chestnut honey in a pastry bag*
· *1 jar of chestnut honey and a honey spoon*

MAKE THE CIGARETTE BATTER FOR THE HONEYCOMB DISKS

Sift the flour. Beat the butter until light and creamy. Beat in the confectioners' sugar, the salt, then the sifted flour, and finally the egg whites. Let the batter rest for at least 1 hour in the refrigerator and then preheat the oven to 325°F (170°C/Gas mark 3), ventilated setting.

Using a spatula, spread the batter thinly over a silicone honeycomb mold placed on a baking sheet and bake in the oven for about 10 minutes. Release the batter edges from the mold as soon as the edges start to color, put it back in the oven for a few minutes, then turn over onto the hot baking sheet. Cut into disks using a plain, round cookie cutter, 4¾ in. (12 cm) in diameter. Return to the oven until a good golden color. As soon as you remove them from the oven, place each disk inside a round-bottomed bowl, 6¼ in. (16 cm) in diameter. Carefully place another bowl, 6¼ in. (16 cm) in diameter, on top.

Allow to cool, turn out carefully and store in a sealed airtight container.

You can keep the rest of the batter for the honey 'something sweet' (the following recipe), in the refrigerator or the freezer.

MAKE THE HONEY ICE CREAM

Bring the milk and UHT cream to a boil and then remove from the heat. Whisk the egg yolks and two honeys in a mixing bowl in a bain-marie at 122°F (50°C) (or in a stand mixer with a temperature-controlled bowl). Add the powdered milk to the hot cream and raise the temperature to 176°F (80°C), using an instant-read thermometer. Remove from the heat, pour this mixture onto the egg yolks and honey, pour into a saucepan and cook over a low-medium heat, stirring as if you were making a crème anglaise. As soon as the cream thickens, strain it through a fine-mesh sieve onto the crème gastronomique, stirring constantly. Pour into a sealed airtight container and keep in the refrigerator. The next day, churn and divide between Pacojet bowls.

MAKE THE MILK FOAM

Soak the gelatin to soften it, squeeze out the leaves and melt in a bowl in a microwave. Add to the rest of the ingredients in the bowl of a stand mixer. Blend everything together, strain through a fine-mesh sieve and transfer it to a large siphon. Add the gas cartridge, charge once and shake well.

MAKE THE SANDED ALMONDS

Roast the almonds for 10 minutes in a 275°F (140°C/Gas mark 1) oven. Make a syrup by bringing the water and sugar to a boil in a copper saucepan. Using an instant read thermometer, bring the temperature to 248°F (120°C) and then add the still-hot almonds. Stir to give them a sandy appearance (that is, they are coated in syrup) and continue to stir until they are caramelized. Add the fleur de sel and, at the end of cooking, the toasted almond oil. Immediately tip onto hot baking sheets and separate the almonds. Keep in a dry place in a sealed airtight container.

MAKE THE PEAR SYRUP

Peel the pears, remove the cores, and cut them into ¾ in. (1.5 cm) cubes. Bring the other ingredients to a boil to make a syrup. Let it cool and then add the pear cubes.

DRESS THE PLATES

Transfer the honey ice cream mixture to the Pacojet.

Chop the caramelized almonds with a knife. Drain the pear cubes on paper towel. Divide them between deep, clover-shaped plates, adding the chopped, caramelized almonds (the equivalent of 3 per plate). Add a spiral of honey ice cream and then pipe the chestnut honey in the pastry bag, following the contour of the spiral. Cover the ice cream in milk foam and then place the cigarette batter honeycomb disks on top.

Prepare the pot of chestnut honey and the honey spoon to drizzle it over the honeycomb in front of your guests.

Recipe photograph, page 127.

Chocolate alveoli

SERVES 8

*Prep: 30 min. (not including time
for making the pastry)
Cook: 8 min.*

**CIGARETTE BATTER
FOR THE HONEYCOMB TUILES**
*See the previous recipe (honey dessert) or
use the batter remaining from that recipe*

CHESTNUT HONEY BUTTER
· ¼ cup (1¾ oz./50 g) butter from Étrez,
  softened
· 3½ tbsp. (2½ oz./75 g) chestnut honey

**MIXTURE FOR THE CHOCOLATE
FLOCKING**
· 4½ oz. (125 g) cocoa butter
· 3½ oz. (110 g) Carúpano dark chocolate
· 1½ oz. (40 g) cacao paste

**MAKE THE CIGARETTE BATTER
FOR THE HONEYCOMB TUILES**
Preheat the oven to 325°F (170°C/Gas
mark 3). Using a rolling pin, spread the
batter over a silicone honeycomb mold
on a baking sheet and with a plain, round
cookie cutter, 2 in. (5 cm) in diameter,
mark out 8 disks. Bake in the oven until
they are a good caramel color (about
7–8 minutes). When they come out of
the oven, place the honeycomb disks
inside half-sphere Flexipan molds, 1½ in.
(4 cm) in diameter. Push the disks down
gently with your fingers. Leave to cool
and harden and then carefully unmold.

MAKE THE CHESTNUT HONEY BUTTER
Thoroughly mix together the softened
butter and honey. Spoon this butter into
a pastry bag fitted with a small, plain tip.
Chill, but do not forget to take it out of
the refrigerator about 1 hour before
decorating the cigarette batter tuiles.

**MAKE THE MIXTURE FOR
THE CHOCOLATE FLOCKING**
Melt all the ingredients together in a
bain-marie and put through a fine-mesh
sieve. Use warm in a velvet spray gun.

TO DRESS THE PLATES
Put the flocking mixture in a velvet spray
gun. Flock the honeycomb tuiles and let
set. Ensure that the pastry bag of honey
butter is at room temperature.

Fill the inside of the tuiles and place
each on a spoon.

Something sweet

Quince

I adore quince. To me it is almost my Proust madeleine. Its fragrance and its colors are unbelievable. It is a fruit that I work with all too rarely: you cannot eat it raw and we don't think about it often enough… I like the grainy texture that stays in the mouth, that rolls under the tongue, and crunches between the teeth. When it is poached, or candied as a paste or jelly, you rediscover that texture, even if it is no longer there. The texture of quince, slightly granular, is something magical.

Dim sum

SERVES 8

Prep: 25 min.
Cook: 4 min.

- 2 cups (500 ml) crème gastronomique from Étrez
- 8 rice spring roll wrappers (buy these in Asian food stores)
- Quince purée (see the following recipe)
- A little vegetable oil for the plates
- Crushed pink peppercorns (coarsely milled)
- ½ cup (120 ml) juice from cooking quince (see the following recipe)

Whip the cream without letting it become grainy but just long enough for it to be firm and light. Spoon it into a pastry bag. Soak the rice spring roll wrappers for 2 minutes in cold water. To assemble the dim sum, drain the wrappers briefly on a cloth. Cut them into squares and pipe a ball of whipped cream in the center of each. Using the pipette of quince purée, pipe it around and over the balls of whipped cream. Fold the dim sum over and cut off the excess rice wrapper.

Very lightly oil the center of 8 shallow dishes and place the dim sum in the dishes. Cover with plastic wrap (cling film) and cook for 3–4 minutes in a steam oven at 190°F (90°C) or in a steamer at gentle heat. When you remove them from the oven or steamer, take off the plastic wrap. Serve dusted with coarsely milled pink peppercorns and accompany with a sauce boat of reheated juice from cooking the quince.

The light touch

I discovered this method with Michel Troisgros. It lets you combine a powerful flavor and a very fragile wrapper in a single mouthful.

The dessert

Poached quince, crystallized walnuts, mint, and whipped cream

SERVES 8

Prep: 1 hr. 30 min.
Rest: 2 hr.
Cook: 5 hr. 15 min.

BLANCMANGE WITH SWISS MINT
· ⅓ oz. (11 g) fresh Swiss mint leaves
· ⅔ cup (5 oz./140 g) fresh egg white (about 5 large whites)
· ½ cup (4 oz.//110 g) superfine sugar
· 1½ sheets (3 g) gelatin

OPALINE SUGAR TUILES WITH WALNUT
· 1¼ cups (8 oz./225 g) superfine sugar
· 8 oz. (225 g) feuilletine (or lacy crepes)
· 1¼ cups (4 oz./110 g) ground walnuts

POACHED QUINCES
· 8 quinces
· 5¼ cups (2¼ lb./1 kg) superfine sugar
· 10 pints (5 liters) water
· 1½ tbsp. (25 ml) lemon juice

QUINCE SAUCE
· 1 tsp. (5 ml) lemon juice
· Scant ½ cup (100 ml) water
· 1 cup (230 ml) juice from cooking the quinces
· ⅔ tsp. (3 ml) quince vinegar
· ½ tsp. (2 g) xanthan gum

MAKE THE BLANCMANGE WITH SWISS MINT
Finely chop the mint without crushing the leaves so as to prevent it turning black and losing its flavor.
Whisk the egg whites, gradually whisking in the sugar, until standing in firm peaks. Soak the gelatin until softened, squeeze excess water from the sheets, and dissolve in a bowl in a microwave. Fold the dissolved gelatin and the chopped mint into the egg whites. Spoon into a pastry bag fitted with a small, plain tip and pipe small balls, ¾ in. (1.5 cm) in diameter, onto a silicone baking mat. Cook them for 3 minutes in a steam oven or a steamer and then keep them in the refrigerator.

MAKE THE OPALINE SUGAR TUILES WITH WALNUT
In a saucepan, heat the sugar until it dissolves and cook to a rich brown caramel. Pour it onto a silicone baking mat placed on a baking sheet and let cool. Blend, leave for 2 hours, and then blend again with the feuilletine and ground walnuts. Keep this mixture in a sealed airtight container.
Preheat the oven to 325°F (175°C/ Gas mark 3) (bakery deck oven/four à sole for professionals). Using a stencil cut to required size, shape this powder into 16 long, thin triangles on a silicone baking mat. Cook them for 5 minutes in the oven. When they come out, using a ring, 9½ in. (24 cm) in diameter, curve the opalines into arc shapes.

POACH THE QUINCES
Peel the quinces, taking care to remove the core, and cut them into eight wedges. Make a syrup by heating the sugar, water, and lemon juice together. Add the quinces, cover the saucepan with a disk of parchment paper the same diameter as the saucepan and cook for about 5 hours over very low heat, without boiling, until the quinces are a beautiful pink color. Allow to cool.

MAKE THE QUINCE SAUCE
Blend all the cold ingredients together. Pour into a pipette and keep chilled.

MAKE THE QUINCE GLAZE
Heat the juice and water together. When the temperature reaches 140°F (60°C), add the pectin-sugar mixture, making sure that it dissolves completely, bring to a boil, and cook for 2 minutes. Strain through a fine-mesh sieve, let cool, and then add the vinegar and eau-de-vie. Use melted, but cold.

MAKE THE CRYSTALLIZED WALNUTS
Make a syrup by bringing the water and sugar to a boil. Let cool to 86°F (30°C). Preheat the oven to 350°F (180°C/ Gas mark 4). Cut the walnuts into thin, well-defined shavings on a mandoline. Using tweezers, dip the best-looking shavings in the syrup and place them on a silicone baking mat. Put them in the oven for 5–10 minutes, until they are a beautiful golden color.

Swiss mint, or Ricqles mint, is a variety of peppermint that is very rich in menthol. It is commonly used in liqueurs, syrups (frosted mint) and bonbons.

Recipe photograph, page 131.

QUINCE GLAZE
· *Generous ¾ cup (200 ml) juice from cooking the quinces*
· *⅓ cup (80 ml) water*
· *1 tsp. (4 g) pectin NH plus ¾ tsp. (4 g) sugar*
· *1 tsp. (5 ml) quince vinegar*
· *¾ tbsp. (12 ml) quince eau-de-vie*

CRYSTALLIZED WALNUTS
· *Scant ½ cup (100 ml) water*
· *⅔ cup (4½ oz./130 g) superfine sugar*
· *15 perfect, well-shaped walnut halves*

WHIPPED CREAM
· *1 cup (250 ml) crème gastronomique from Étrez*
· *½ cup (125 ml) UHT whipping cream*

TO DRESS THE PLATES
Very carefully, slice some of the poached quince wedges into evenly shaped ribbons, so they look visually attractive (you will need between 10 and 12 ribbons for each serving). Check that the fruits are cooked and have kept their shape, taking care to reserve the remaining poached quinces to make the quince purée. Also make sure to trim the base of some of the ribbons so that you can put quenelles of whipped cream there. Glaze the quince ribbons with the quince glaze.

Make the quince purée by blending some of the remaining poached quinces in a Thermomix, adding a little of the cooking juice, if necessary. Spoon this purée into a pastry bag fitted with a plain tip, ¾ in. (1.5 cm) in diameter.

Whip the two creams together until their texture is firm but light. Place an opaline triangle on each serving plate and then about 7 mint blancmanges within. Place a second opaline on the other side of the blancmanges, adding a little piped quince purée that will also stick the opaline to the blancmanges. Place the glazed quince shavings attractively on the blancmanges. Decorate with the crystallized walnuts and then, using a coffee spoon, garnish with 5 quenelles of whipped cream.

Using a Microplane®, grate crystallized walnuts over the desserts and finish with the quince sauce.

Quince jelly

SERVES 8
Prep: 20 min.
Rest: 1 hr.
Cook: 1 min.

QUINCE JELLY
· *2 cups (500 ml) cooking juice from the quinces (see previous recipe)*
· *¾ tsp (3 g) Kappa®*

TO SERVE
· *½ cup (120 ml) crème gastronomique from Étrez*

MAKE THE QUINCE JELLY
Heat the quince cooking juice, add the Kappa® and boil for 1 minute. Stretch plastic wrap (cling film) around the side of a rectangular baking frame. Strain the juice mixture through a fine-mesh sieve and pour it into the frame to a depth of ¾ in. (1.5 cm). Allow to cool and set.

TO FINISH
Cut the quince jelly into 8 mouthfuls using a round cookie cutter, 1 in. (2.5 cm) in diameter. Using a melon baller, ½ in. (1 cm) in diameter, hollow out the center of each jelly.
· Spoon the *crème gastronomique* into a pastry bag and pipe an attractive swirl in each jelly hollow.

Something sweet

FEASTS
GREAT AND
SMALL AROUND
THE CLOCK

LITTLE HAZELNUT BOATS

In the words of

FRANÇOIS PERRET

I like *patisserie* that doesn't take itself too seriously. With these little 'boats', we are browsing the packets of those *classic* small cakes on supermarket shelves and, as a result, it is rather fun to rediscover those novelties from *childhood tea parties*. Rich, buttery Breton shortbread, the taste of roasted hazelnuts and gianduja milk chocolate: it is difficult to think of another recipe that is more of a trip down memory lane or more unifying. You are *coming out of school*, it's *four o'clock* and time for cake. It is almost the one tiny weakness you will be unable to resist. At the Ritz Paris it forms part of the *selection of friandises* that welcomes you when you arrive in your room. And, when you leave, you slip it into your travel bag, like a *delectable little talisman*.

Little hazelnut boats

SERVES 8–10

Prep: 40 min.
Cook: 12 min

BRETON BUTTER SHORTBREAD
- *1 cup plus 2 tbsp. (5 oz./150 g) all-purpose flour*
- *½ tsp. (2 g) baking powder*
- *Scant 1 cup (7 oz./200 g) butter, softened*
- *Scant ⅓ cup (3 oz./80 g) confectioners' sugar*
- *1 egg yolk*
- *1 oz. (30 g) ground almonds*

GIANDUJA SAUCE
- *5 oz. (150 g) gianduja milk chocolate spread*
- *1 oz. (30 g) Tannea milk chocolate, 43% cacao*

MAKE THE BRETON BUTTER SHORTBREAD

Sift the flour and baking powder together. Preheat the oven to 325°F (170°C/Gas mark 3).

In the bowl of a stand mixer fitted with the paddle, mix the softened butter and confectioners' sugar together on low speed until they are light and creamy. Add the egg yolk and then mix in the sifted flour and baking powder, followed finally by the ground almonds. Take care the whole time not to introduce air into the mixture: do all the mixing on the lowest speed possible.

Transfer the dough to a pastry bag fitted with a plain no. 8 tip and pipe ⅓ oz. (10 g) into each cavity of a Flexipan boat mold. Bake for about 12 minutes in the oven. Halfway through the baking time, push down the center of each shortbread with the back of a spoon to create an oval dip in the shortbread that is identical in shape to the mold and with a border that is an even width all the way round.

MAKE THE GIANDUJA SAUCE

Melt the ingredients to a maximum of 104°F (40°C), using an instant-read thermometer to check the temperature. Leave to cool a little and then fill the middle of each boat with the still warm sauce. Allow to firm up.

Little caramel boats

I created a special mold specifically for this recipe but here I've adapted it so that you can make it in a 10¼-in. (26-cm), 1¾ in. (4.5 cm) deep cake ring. "Exhausted" vanilla powder is produced by drying the vanilla beans after they have been split and their seeds scraped out, before they are ground to a very fine powder. Sift the powder and store it in a small glass jar sealed with an airtight lid. Before pouring over the sauce, you can decorate the top of each boat with a little edible gold leaf, the reflections of which will shimmer through the caramel.

SERVES 8–10

Prep: 1 hr. 30 min.
Rest: 3 hr.
Cook: 35 min.

SWEET SHORTCRUST PASTRY CRUMB
· ⅔ cup (3 oz./90 g) confectioners' sugar
· ½ cup (4½ oz./130 g) butter from Étrez, diced and softened
· 1 oz. (30 g) ground almonds
· 1 egg
· 1 pinch (0.5 g) fleur de sel
· 1 pinch (0.5 g) "exhausted" vanilla powder
· 2 cups (9 oz./250 g) all-purpose flour

VANILLA MOUSSE
· 3½ sheets (7 g) gelatin
· 1 Bourbon vanilla bean
· Generous 1 cup (270 ml) whipping cream
· ⅓ cup (2½ oz./70 g) superfine sugar
· ⅓ cup (3 oz./90 g) egg yolk (4½ large yolks)
· 1¼ cups (300 ml) whipping cream, whipped

CHEESECAKE BASE
· 10½ oz. (300 g) sweet shortcrust pastry crumb
· 1½ tbsp. (¾ oz./20 g) dry butter, 84% butterfat

MAKE THE SWEET SHORTCRUST PASTRY CRUMB
In a stand mixer, beat together the confectioners' sugar, butter, and ground almonds. Add the egg, fleur de sel, and vanilla powder. Incorporate the flour and mix gently until you have a smooth dough. Wrap in plastic wrap (cling film), chill in the refrigerator for 1 hour, and then roll out ¹⁄₁₆ in. (2 mm) thick. Preheat the oven to 325°F (160°C/Gas mark 3) and heat a baking sheet. Lift the pastry onto the hot baking sheet and bake until lightly golden (about 20 minutes). Leave to cool, break into pieces and then blend to a fine powder. Store in a dry place in a sealed airtight container.

MAKE THE VANILLA MOUSSE
Soak the gelatin in cold water. Slit the vanilla bean lengthwise, scrape out the seeds and then cut the bean into small pieces. In a saucepan, bring the cream to a boil with the vanilla, remove from the heat, cover and let infuse for 15 minutes. Whisk the sugar with the egg yolks until pale and thick and then add the hot cream, a little at a time, whisking continuously. Return the mixture to the saucepan and cook over a low heat, stirring with a spatula. When the cream thickens, remove the vanilla, and process with an immersion blender. Strain through a fine-mesh sieve, add the squeezed out gelatin and allow to cool before folding in the whipped cream.

MAKE THE CHEESECAKE BASE
Preheat the oven to 325°F (170°C/Gas mark 3), ventilated setting. Using a stand mixer fitted with a paddle attachment, mix the powdered shortcrust pastry with the dry butter until combined. Spread the mixture out in a 9½ in. (24 cm) cake ring placed on a baking sheet and then pat it down in an even layer. Bake for about 7 minutes in the oven, allow to cool in the ring and then store in the refrigerator.

CARAMEL FILLING
- 1 cup (6½ oz./180 g) superfine sugar
- 1 oz. (25 g) glucose syrup DE40
- 1⅓ cups (320 ml) heavy cream
- 1 pinch (0.5 g) "exhausted" vanilla powder
- ¼ cup (3 oz./80 g) egg yolk (4 large yolks)
- ¼ cup (1¾ oz./50 g) lightly-salted butter, softened

FLAN PASTRY
- ⅔ cup (5¼ oz./80 g) lightly salted butter, softened
- ⅓ cup (1¾ oz./50 g) confectioners' sugar
- 1½ tbsp. (1 oz./25 g) egg yolk (about 1 large yolk)
- 1 cup plus 1 tbsp. (5 oz./140 g) all-purpose flour
- ¾ oz. (20 g) ground almonds
- Cocoa butter, melted

FLOATING ISLAND CARAMEL
- 1 cup (7 oz./200 g) superfine sugar
- ½ cup (110 ml) hot water

WHITE CHOCOLATE VELVET SPRAY
- 7 oz. (200 g) white chocolate
- 7 oz. (200 g) cocoa butter
- 1 pinch (0.5 g) "exhausted" vanilla powder

MAKE THE CARAMEL FILLING
Heat the sugar and glucose syrup in a saucepan, without adding any water, until you have a rich, dark, lightly smoking caramel. It is important to continue cooking the caramel to this stage. Bring the cream, vanilla powder, and salt to a boil and then pour onto the caramel in order to dissolve it. Lightly whisk the egg yolks and, very gradually, add the caramel, mixing well: be careful not to cook the yolks. Cook, stirring continuously to make a crème anglaise. Strain through a fine-mesh sieve and let cool to between 104–95 °F (40–35°C) before adding the softened butter and then pouring the mixture over the cheesecake base in the ring. Freeze for 3 hours.

MAKE THE FLAN PASTRY
Preheat the oven to 325 °F (160 °C/Gas mark 3), ventilated setting. In the bowl of a stand mixer, beat the butter until it is soft and creamy. Add, in the following order, the confectioners' sugar, egg yolk, flour, and ground almonds to make a soft dough. Roll out the dough $^1/_{16}$ in. (2 mm) thick and cut out a disk, 11 in. (28 cm) in diameter. Bake for 10 minutes in the oven between two silicone baking mats. When it comes out of the oven, brush the pastry with cocoa butter to seal it.

MAKE THE FLOATING ISLAND CARAMEL
Heat the sugar until it is a golden brown caramel and then prevent further cooking by adding the hot water. Cool and store in the refrigerator.

TO ASSEMBLE
Stretch plastic wrap (cling film) over one side of a 10¼ in. (26 cm) ring and fit a strip of food-grade acetate, 1¾ in. (4.5 cm) deep, inside the ring around the sides. Assemble the dessert in reverse order: fill the ring with vanilla mousse until three-quarters full, taking care the mousse reaches right to the edges of the ring. Fit the cheesecake base on top, caramel side down. Smooth the surface and then place in the freezer.

Just before unmolding, melt the velvet spray ingredients and pour into a velvet spray gun. Unmold, remove the acetate strip and spray the dessert. Place it, cheesecake base down, on a serving plate and top with the floating island caramel sauce in front of your guests.

Recipe photographs, following pages.

SERVES 8–10

Prep: 15 min. (not including infusing and caramelizing)
Cook: 50 min.

· *1 vanilla bean*
· *Generous 1 cup (270 ml) milk*
· *⅔ cup (6 oz./170 g) egg yolk (about 8½ large yolks)*
· *½ cup (4 oz./110 g) superfine sugar*
· *3 cups (750 ml) chilled whipping cream*
· *Brown sugar for the caramelization*
· *Confectioners' sugar and a stencil, to decorate*

Preheat the oven to 190°F (90°C/Gas on lowest setting). Slit the vanilla bean lengthwise and scrape out the seeds. Bring the milk to a boil with the vanilla bean and seeds. Cover and let infuse.

Whisk the egg yolks and sugar together until pale and thick. Pour the milk over the yolks and sugar, whisking constantly, add the chilled whipping cream and strain through a fine-mesh sieve. Take care not to incorporate any air into the mixture while you are preparing it. Pour the mixture into ½ cup (125 ml) molds, doing this close to the oven to avoid the molds overflowing as you put them in the oven. Cook for 45–50 minutes: the crème is cooked when it is set in the center. The cooking time may vary depending on the shape of the molds used.

To caramelize, gently dab a piece of paper towel over the surface of each crème to blot any moisture. Remove the paper and dust the top of each with sifted brown sugar.

Caramelize the sugar with a gas gun, starting at the outside and working towards the center. Dust again with brown sugar and caramelize once more. Decorate by placing your chosen stencil on top and dusting over confectioners' sugar.

Vanilla
— crème brûlée —

VANILLA MERINGUE

In the words of

FRANÇOIS PERRET

This is a *fundamental dessert*, in the sense that it brings together the essentials of patisserie, the steps I took one by one toward making my first cakes as an apprentice: meringue, *crème pâtissière* (pastry cream), and whipped cream. These *three great cornerstones* of professional bakeries and homemade desserts are loved by all the world—and me most of all. For the *Bar Vendôme*, the beating heart of the hotel where patisserie has its place all day long, I decided to bring them together in a single cloud of *reassuring sweetness*. Once again "size matters" but haven't I already told you that? In my eyes, *minimalism* is the complete opposite of treating yourself. I like callipygian desserts, but with a *light soul*. Here, apart from the meringue, no extra sugar has been added, which is no reason not to come and eat the dessert. I use it *sparingly*, as a seasoning to sharpen the flavors. Eating must never tip over into that uncomfortable feeling of having overindulged.

Vanilla meringue

You can make the meringue domes in advance and store them in a dry place in a sealed airtight container.

SERVES 6

Prep: 1 hr. 30 min.
Cook: 1 hr. 45 min.

FRENCH MERINGUE
· *Scant 2 cups (14 oz./400 g) egg white*
  (about 13 large whites)
· *2 cups (14 oz./400 g) superfine sugar*
· *3 cups (14 oz./400 g) confectioners' sugar*

VANILLA CAVIAR
· *¾ sheet (1.5 g) gelatin*
· *15 vanilla beans*
· *⅓ cup (75 ml) water*
· *½ cup (3½ oz./100 g) superfine sugar*

CRÈME PÂTISSIÈRE
· *1 vanilla bean*
· *1¾ cups (400 ml) UHT whole milk*
· *1 tbsp. (14 g) butter, diced*
· *Generous ¼ cup (2 oz./55 g)*
  superfine sugar
· *¼ cup (2⅓ oz./65 g) egg yolk*
  (about 3 large yolks)
· *Scant ¼ cup (1 oz./25 g) cornstarch*

TO ASSEMBLE
· *1¼ cups (300 ml) whipping*
  cream, 33% butterfat
· *Generous ¾ cup (200 ml)*
  crème gastronomique from Étrez
· *Cocoa butter*
· *"Exhausted" vanilla bean powder*

MAKE THE FRENCH MERINGUE

Preheat the oven to 160°F (70°C/Gas on lowest setting), ventilated setting. In a stand mixer, beat the egg whites, gradually adding the superfine sugar to make a stiff meringue. Fold in the confectioners' sugar using a flexible spatula. Shape a little of the meringue into a dome by spooning it into a ladle, 4 in. (10 cm) in diameter. Smooth level and then, using a small flexible spatula, carefully release the dome of meringue from the ladle onto a baking sheet lined with parchment paper. Make sure the dome holds its shape but pull up a few hedgehog-like spikes over the rounded surface. Repeat using the remaining mixture to make 10 meringue domes. Bake them in the oven for 1 hour 15 minutes and then hollow out each dome at the base with a spoon. Place the domes back on the baking sheet, base side up, and return them to the oven for a further 1 hour 30 minutes to dry out completely.

MAKE THE VANILLA CAVIAR

Soak the gelatin in cold water for 10 minutes. Slit the vanilla beans, scrape out the seeds and cut the beans into small pieces. Bring the water and sugar to a boil, add the vanilla beans and seeds and then blend them until fine. Pour the mixture into a fine-mesh sieve and scrape with the back of a spoon to push the maximum amount you can through the sieve. Add the squeezed-out gelatin, mix it in, and then let cool. The texture of the caviar must be sticky and elastic.

MAKE THE CRÈME PÂTISSIÈRE

Slit the vanilla bean and scrape out the seeds. Bring the milk to a boil in a saucepan with the butter, 1 tbsp.(15 g) of the sugar. Whisk the egg yolks with the rest of the sugar until pale. Add the cornstarch and then a little of the hot milk. Stir until combined, pour the mixture back into the saucepan and bring to a boil, stirring constantly. After 2 minutes boiling, pour it onto a baking sheet lined with plastic wrap (cling film) and cool quickly. Weigh out 1 lb. 2 oz. (500 g) of the crème pâtissière for the 10 meringues.

TO ASSEMBLE

Whip the two creams together to soft peaks.
Create a seal inside the meringue shells by brushing them with melted cocoa butter and then fill each shell in the following order with: 1½ oz. (40 g) whipped cream, ⅓ oz. (10 g) vanilla caviar and, finally, about 1¾ oz. (50 g) crème pâtissière. Smooth the surface of each and place the meringues, flat side down, on serving plates. Decorate by dusting with vanilla powder.

Pomelo cheesecake

I use Coquibresse, a soft cheese that I have sent to me from a cooperative creamery in Bresse. Alternatively, use cream cheese.

SERVES 8–10

Prep: 1 hr.
Rest: 1 hr.
Cook: 22 min.

GRAPEFRUIT MARMALADE
· 2 grapefruit (for 2½ oz. 75 g zest
  and 8 oz./230 g flesh)
· 1 sheet (2 g) gelatin
· Scant ½ cup (3 oz./90 g) superfine sugar
· ⅔ tsp. (3 g) yellow pectin

CHEESECAKE MOUSSE
· 2½ sheets (5 g) gelatin
· ¾ cup (6¾ oz./190 g) coquibresse
  or cream cheese
· ⅓ cup (2¼ oz./65 g) superfine sugar
· 1 cup (235 ml) whipping cream
· 4½ tsp. (12 g) confectioners' sugar

PINK GRAPEFRUIT ICING
· 7 sheets (14 g) gelatin
· 8 oz. (230 g) white chocolate, chopped
· 3½ oz. (110 g) sweetened condensed milk
· Scant ⅔ cup (4¼ oz./120 g) superfine sugar
· 8 oz. (220 g) glucose syrup
· ⅔ cup (160 ml) grapefruit juice
· 4 tbsp. (60 ml) water
· 2 or 3 drops of grenadine syrup

MAKE THE GRAPEFRUIT MARMALADE
Remove the zest from the grapefruits using a vegetable peeler, peeling away only the zest and not the pith. Blanch the zest three times, draining after each blanching and continuing with fresh cold water. Drain.

Soak the gelatin in cold water.

Peel the pith and membranes from the grapefruit (as you do this, collect any juice that runs out and save it for the icing) and then coarsely chop the grapefruit flesh. Mix the sugar and pectin together and cook it with the flesh and zest of the grapefruit. Boil for 5 minutes, process with an immersion blender and cook for around 5 minutes until the mixture has the consistency of marmalade. Add the squeezed out gelatin sheet and pour into a shallow tray to make a layer, ¼ in. (5 mm) thick. Allow to set and then cut out ten 2 in. (5 cm) squares. Keep the marmalade squares in the refrigerator as they will be the filling for the cheesecake mousse.

MAKE THE CHEESECAKE MOUSSE
Soak the gelatin for 10 minutes in cold water. Melt the coquibresse with the superfine sugar in a bain-marie. Add the squeezed-out gelatin sheets. Whip the cream with the confectioners' sugar to soft peaks. Combine the two mixtures and divide it between ten 2.5 in. (6 cm) square frames, ¾ in. (2 cm) deep. Place a square of grapefruit marmalade in the center of each mousse and smooth the surface level. Store in the freezer.

SWEET SHORTCRUST PASTRY CRUMB
· ⅔ cup (3 oz./90 g) confectioners' sugar
· ½ cup (4½ oz./130 g) lightly salted butter, softened
· 1 oz. (30 g) ground almonds
· 1 egg
· "Exhausted" vanilla bean powder (see page 140)
· 2 cups (9 oz./250 g) all-purpose flour

CHEESECAKE BASE
· 13 oz. (370 g) sweet shortcrust pastry made into a powder
· 2 tbsp. (1 oz./25 g) dry butter, 84% butterfat

TO FINISH
· 1 Chinese pomelo

MAKE THE PINK GRAPEFRUIT ICING

Soak the gelatin sheets in cold water for 10 minutes. Put the chopped white chocolate, sweetened condensed milk, and squeezed-out gelatin sheets in a large bowl.

Heat the sugar, glucose syrup, grapefruit juice, and water to 217°F (103°C), using an instant-read thermometer to check the temperature. Pour this into the white chocolate mixture, mixing carefully and adding a few drops of grenadine syrup to obtain the desired shade of pink. Process with an immersion blender, cover and store in the refrigerator. Any icing left over after assembling the cheesecake can be stored in the freezer to use for another recipe.

MAKE THE SWEET SHORTCRUST PASTRY CRUMB

Mix together the confectioners' sugar, softened butter, and ground almonds. Add the egg and powdered vanilla. Incorporate the flour and mix lightly to make a smooth dough. Wrap the dough in plastic wrap (cling film) and chill in the refrigerator for 1 hour. Take 1 lb. (450 g) of this dough and roll it ¹⁄₁₆ in. (2 mm) thick. Keep the rest of the dough in the freezer for another recipe. Preheat the oven to 325°F (160°C/Gas mark 3), place the dough on a baking sheet and bake until pale golden (about 10–15 minutes). Allow to cool and then reduce to a powder in a food processor.

MAKE THE CHEESECAKE BASE

In a stand mixer fitted with the paddle, mix together the powdered short-crust pastry and the dry butter until combined. Roll the dough about ½ in. (1 cm) thick and line it into 2½ in. (6 cm) square frames. Preheat the oven to 325°F (170°C/Gas mark 3) and bake for about 7 minutes. Remove the frames and cool the bases on a baking sheet in the refrigerator.

TO FINISH

Unmold the cheesecake mousses onto a wire rack. Melt the grapefruit icing, ensuring that it melts but remains cold. Ice the mousses on the rack using a spatula and then fit them on top of the bases.

Peel the Chinese pomelo and remove the skin from the segments so you are left with just the flesh. Flake the flesh and place a generous amount on top of each mousse.

The floating island
— *that does not float* —

SERVES 8–10

Prep: 2 hr.
Cook: 1 hr.

MILK FOR IMBIBING
· *1 Bourbon vanilla bean*
· *1¼ cups (300 ml) whole milk*
· *2½ tbsp. (1 oz./30 g) superfine sugar*

ALMOND SAVOY SPONGE
· *2 oz. (50 g) slivered almonds*
· *⅔ cup (5⅔ oz./160 g) egg*
  (about 3 large eggs)
· *¾ cup (5 oz./145 g) superfine sugar*
· *⅓ cup (3 oz./80 g) butter, plus extra*
  for the ring
· *1 cup (3½ oz./100 g) cake flour*
  (type T45), plus extra for the ring
· *cup (2 oz./55 g) potato flour*
· *1 tsp. (5 g) baking powder*

CRÈME BRÛLÉE FILLING
· *1 Bourbon vanilla bean*
· *⅓ cup (3 oz./80 g) egg yolk*
  (about 4 large yolks)
· *3¾ tbsp. (1½ oz./45 g) superfine sugar*
· *2 tbsp. plus 2 tsp. (40 ml) milk*
· *Generous ¾ cup (200 ml) UHT*
  whipping cream

CARAMEL DECORATION
· *1 cup (7 oz./200 g) superfine sugar*
· *½ cup (110 ml) hot water*

PREPARE THE MILK FOR IMBIBING

Slit the vanilla bean lengthwise and scrape out the seeds. In a saucepan, bring the vanilla bean, vanilla seeds, milk, and sugar to a boil. Set aside but keep hot.

MAKE THE ALMOND SAVOY SPONGE

Toast the slivered almonds on a baking sheet for about 8 minutes in a 300°C (150°C/Gas mark 2) oven. Remove the almonds from the baking sheet and let cool. Increase the oven temperature to 325°F (160°C/Gas mark 3), ventilated setting.

In a stand mixer, whisk the eggs with the sugar. Melt the butter and add it while still hot. Sift the flour, potato flour, and baking powder together, switch off the mixer and, using a flexible spatula, fold the dry ingredients into the whisked eggs–butter–sugar. Lightly butter and flour a tart ring, 9½ in. (23 cm) in diameter set on a baking sheet. Spread an even layer of toasted almonds in the ring and then pour the sponge batter on top to reach one-third of the height of the ring. Bake for 20 minutes in the oven. Unmold the sponge while it is still warm and spoon the imbibing milk over it to moisten it completely. Let cool and then put in the freezer.

MAKE THE CRÈME BRÛLÉE FILLING

Preheat the oven to 190°F (90°C/Gas on lowest setting), ventilated setting. Slit the vanilla bean lengthwise and scrape out the seeds. Whisk the egg yolks and sugar together until pale and thick. Bring the milk and cream to a boil with the vanilla seeds and then pour onto the beaten eggs. Line a tart ring, 9½ in. (23 cm) in diameter, with plastic wrap (cling film) suitable for use in a low oven, and pour the crème brûlée mixture into it. Cook for 35 minutes in the oven. Cool and then let the filling firm up in the refrigerator before unmolding it.

MAKE THE CARAMEL DECORATION

Cook the sugar until it is a rich red-brown caramel and then halt the cooking process by adding the hot water.

CARAMEL MOUSSE
· 4 sheets (8 g) gelatin
· 1 Bourbon vanilla bean
· Scant 1 cup (220 ml) UHT whipping cream
· Scant 1 cup (6⅓ oz./180 g) superfine sugar
· 1 oz. (30 g) glucose syrup
· 2 cups (500 ml) whipped cream

EGG WHITES WHISKED TO A SNOW
· 1½ sheets (3 g) gelatin
· ⅔ cup (5¼ oz./150 g) egg white (about 5 large egg whites)
· ½ cup (3½ oz./110 g) superfine sugar

POWDERED CARAMEL
· Scant 1¼ cups (8 oz./225 g) superfine sugar
· 1¾ oz. (50 g) cold butter, diced
· 1½ tbsp. (¾ oz./20 g) cocoa butter, melted and still hot

MAKE THE CARAMEL MOUSSE
Soak the gelatin in cold water. Slit the vanilla bean lengthwise and scrape out the seeds. Bring the cream to a boil with the vanilla bean and seeds and take off the heat. Cook the sugar and the glucose syrup to a rich red-brown caramel and then halt the cooking process with the hot cream and vanilla. Squeeze excess water from the gelatin and add. Strain through a fine-mesh sieve, let cool and then fold in the whipped cream with a flexible spatula. Spoon the mousse into a pastry bag and keep chilled.

PREPARE THE EGG WHITES WHISKED TO A SNOW
Soak the gelatin in cold water. Meanwhile, whisk the egg whites in a stand mixer, gradually adding the sugar but not letting the whites become too firm. Squeeze out the gelatin and melt it in a bowl in a microwave. Add it to the whisked whites. Lightly oil a tart ring, 10¼ in. (26 cm) in diameter and ¾ in. (2 cm) deep. Spread the mixture into it and cook in a steam oven at 176°F (80°C) for 3 minutes.

MAKE THE POWDERED CARAMEL
Cook the sugar until it is a rich red-brown caramel. Halt the cooking process by adding the butter a little at a time, followed by the cocoa butter. Pour onto a silicone baking mat, let cool, and then blend to a fine powder. Keep dry in a sealed airtight container.

TO ASSEMBLE
Stretch plastic wrap (cling film) over a round pastry ring, 10¼ in. (26 cm) in diameter, 1¾ in. (4.5 cm) deep, and place it, plastic wrap down, on a board. Line the sides of the ring with a band of food-grade acetate, 1¾ in. (4.5 cm) high. Spread a thin layer of caramel mousse over the frozen sponge. Smooth with a spatula and then add the crème brûlée filling, positioning it in the middle of the mousse.

Fill the ring to halfway with caramel mousse, taking great care to spread the mousse right to the sides of the ring. Put the sponge in the center, crème brûlée filling down. Spread over the remaining mousse in a smooth layer with a spatula and store in the refrigerator.

Once the dessert is firm, unmold it and let it start to come to room temperature so that the powder will stick well. Coat with the caramel powder and place the egg white snow on top. Finish by decorating the snow with liquid caramel, either using a piping cone or a spoon. You can also add slivered almonds if you wish.

Recipe photographs, following pages.

Raspberry Charlotte

SERVES 10

Prep: 50 min.
Cook: 1 hr. 20 min.

LIGHT SAVOY SPONGE CAKE
· *1 cup plus 1 tbsp. (5 oz./145 g) cake flour*
  (type T45)
· *½ cup (2½ oz./75 g) potato flour*
· *1¼ tsp. (6 g) baking powder*
· *½ cup (4 oz./112 g) butter*
· *Scant 1 cup (7 oz./220 g) egg*
  (about 4 large eggs)
· *1 cup (7 oz./200 g) superfine sugar*

RASPBERRY IMBIBING SYRUP
· *½ cup (125 ml) water*
· *2½ tbsp. (1 oz./30 g) superfine sugar*
· *½ tsp. (2 ml) raspberry vinegar*
· *½ tsp. (2 ml) raspberry eau-de-vie*

RASPBERRY JUICE
· *1 lb. 2oz. (500 g) frozen raspberries*
· *Scant ¼ cup (1¾ oz./50 g) brown sugar*

RASPBERRY CONSERVE
· *Strained raspberries (from the previous*
  step for making the juice)
· *Sugar*
· *4 tsp. (20 ml) lemon juice*

MAKE THE LIGHT SAVOY SPONGE CAKE
Preheat the oven to 325°F (160°C/Gas mark 3), ventilated setting. Sift the flour, potato flour, and baking powder together. Melt the butter. In a stand mixer, whisk the eggs with the sugar. Add the hot melted butter (the temperature is important) and then fold in the sifted dry ingredients with a flexible spatula. Transfer the batter to a pastry bag. Butter and flour 10 individual Parisienne brioche (brioche à tête) Flexipan® molds and pipe 2 oz. (55 g) batter into each. Bake in the oven for 14 minutes. When the sponges come out of the oven, cover them, still in their molds, with a sheet of parchment paper and then place a board on top and let rest for 10 minutes to flatten the surface. Unmold while still warm.

MAKE THE RASPBERRY IMBIBING SYRUP
Bring the water and the superfine sugar to a boil. Allow to cool and then add the vinegar and raspberry eau-de-vie. Set aside.

MAKE THE RASPBERRY JUICE
Put all the ingredients in a round-bottomed bowl in a bain-marie. Cover with plastic wrap (cling film) and heat for 1 hour. Strain through a fine-mesh sieve without pressing down on the fruit. Put the juice in the refrigerator and keep the raspberries for making the conserve.

MAKE THE RASPBERRY CONSERVE
Weigh the raspberries reserved from straining the juice and add 60% of their weight in sugar. Add the lemon juice and carefully mix everything together. Pour into a saucepan and bring to a boil over high heat. Cook for 3 minutes, stirring constantly. Pour the conserve into jam pots and store in the refrigerator.

Recipe photograph, previous page.

RASPBERRY COMPOTE
· 3½ oz. (100 g) fresh raspberries
· 2 oz. (60 g) raspberry conserve

RASPBERRY CREAM SAUCE
· ⅓ cup (5½ tbsp./80 ml) raspberry juice
· ¼ cup (1 oz./32 g) confectioners' sugar
· 1⅓ cups (320 ml) crème gastronomique
  from Étrez, 40% butterfat

MAKE THE RASPBERRY COMPOTE
Crush the fresh raspberries with a fork and then mix them with the conserve.

MAKE THE RASPBERRY CREAM SAUCE
Mix the raspberry juice and confectioners' sugar together. Add the cream, mixing it in with a flexible spatula. Strain through a fine sieve and keep in the refrigerator until ready to serve.

TO ASSEMBLE AND FINISH
Using a 1⅓ in. (3.5 cm) cookie cutter, cut a round from the top of each sponge, centering the cutter and making a neat hollow, ¾ in. (2 cm) deep. Using a brush, moisten the sponges with the imbibing syrup and then dust them generously with confectioners' sugar before placing them in a 425°F (220°C/Gas mark 7) oven (non-ventilated setting) for 4–5 minutes. When they come out of the oven, dust the sponges again with confectioners' sugar and allow to cool.

Fill the raspberries with raspberry compote. Pile them generously on top of each sponge (using 1¾–2 oz./50–55 g filled raspberries for each). Serve the raspberry cream sauce separately.

Pear
— in a cage —

SERVES 8–10

Prep: 1 hr.
Cook: about 1 hr. 30 min.

FLOURLESS CHOCOLATE SPONGE CAKE
· *2½ oz. (75 g) Carúpano chocolate,*
  70% cacao solids
· *2 oz. (50 g) cacao paste*
· *Scant 1 cup (7¾ oz./220 g) egg yolk*
  (about 11 large yolks)
· *Scant 1 cup (6¾ oz./190 g) egg white*
  (about 6 large whites)
· *¾ cup (5¼ oz./150 g) superfine sugar*

POACHING SYRUP AND PEARS
· *1 vanilla bean*
· *8½ cups (2 liters) water*
· *2¾ cups (1 lb. 5 oz./600 g) brown sugar*
· *8 Williams pears*
· *¾ tsp. (3 g) ascorbic acid*

PAN-FRIED PEARS
· *1 lb. 2 oz. (500 g) fresh pears*
  (to make 12 oz./350 g peeled, cored
  and cubed fruit)
· *1 tbsp. (½ oz./15 g) brown sugar*
· *½ vanilla bean with the seeds scraped out*
· *4 tsp. (20 ml) pear eau-de-vie*

MAKE THE FLOURLESS CHOCOLATE SPONGE CAKE
Preheat the oven to 300°F (150°C/Gas mark 2). Chop the chocolate and melt it in a bain-marie with the cacao paste to 104°F (40°C). Whisk the egg yolks and egg whites together with the sugar. Fold in the chocolate. Fill 10 ungreased (this is important) Flexipan molds, 2.5 in. (6 cm) deep and 2.5 in. (6 cm) in diameter with this mixture. Bake for 14 minutes in the oven and then allow to cool in the molds.

MAKE THE SYRUP AND POACH THE PEARS
Slit the vanilla bean lengthwise and scrape out the seeds. Put the vanilla bean, seeds, water, and brown sugar in a saucepan and bring to a boil. Set aside to infuse, strain the warm syrup through a fine-mesh sieve and let cool completely.

Peel the pears without removing their stalks and cut a slice from the base of each so the pears stand upright. Each pear must be 2.5 in. (6 cm) tall, not including its stalk. Remove the cores with a 1 in. (2.5 cm) cookie cutter. Shave the pears using a Microplane® grater to ensure each one has a smooth, even shape. As you peel and remove the core from each pear immerse it in a bowl of cold water to which ice cubes and the ascorbic acid have been added. Keep the pear trimmings in the bowl of acidulated water as well.

To poach the pears, drain them from the bowl of water and put them in a saucepan. Heat the syrup to 176°F (80°C) and pour it over the pears. Press a circle of parchment paper, the same size as the diameter of the saucepan, over the surface and then leave to poach over a gentle heat for about 30 minutes, without letting the syrup simmer or boil, until the pears have a melt-in-the-mouth texture but still keep their shape.

PAN-FRY THE PEARS
Drain the pear trimmings and cut them into cubes of about ½ in. (1 cm). In a skillet, cook them for a few moments with the brown sugar and vanilla. Flambé with the eau-de-vie and, if necessary, add water to finish cooking them. They must still be firm.

CHOCOLATE MOUSSE

- 1¼ sheets (2.5 g) gelatin
- 7 oz. (195 g) Sambirano dark chocolate
- ¾ cup (180 ml) whipping cream
- 4 egg yolks
- ¼ cup (1½ oz./45 g) superfine sugar
- Scant 1 cup (6⅓ oz./180 g) egg white (about 6 large whites)

CHOCOLATE DECORATION

- 2½ oz. (75 g) Carúpano chocolate, 70% cacao solids

CHOCOLATE SAUCE

- 2 oz. (60 g) Carúpano chocolate, 70% cacao solids
- 2 oz. (60 g) Samara chocolate, 62% ganache
- ½ oz. (15 g) milk chocolate
- Generous ¾ cup (200 ml) milk
- Generous ¾ cup (200 ml) whipping cream

TO FINISH

- 10½ oz. (300 g) neutral glaze

MAKE THE CHOCOLATE MOUSSE

Soak the gelatin in cold water. Melt the chocolate in a bain-marie to 122°F (50°C). Whip the cream (it must be just holding its shape but not be too firm) and keep it in the refrigerator. Whisk the egg yolks with ½ oz. (15 g) of the sugar to a sabayon. Meanwhile, using another beater, whisk the egg whites to soft peaks, adding the remaining 1 oz. (30 g) sugar to stiffen them. Using a whisk, mix in the melted chocolate with half the cream and half the sabayon, finishing the process with a flexible spatula. Squeeze out the gelatin, melt the sheets in a microwave oven and incorporate into the mousse.

MAKE THE CHOCOLATE DECORATION

Temper the chocolate by melting it in a bain-marie to about 122°F (50°C) and then let the overall temperature drop quickly to 81°F (27°C) (not just the temperature of the chocolate at the bottom). Reheat to raise the temperature gradually to a maximum of 88–90 °F (31–32°C) to liquify it. Pour the chocolate onto an acetate sheet, smooth into a thin, even layer and then scrape a chocolate comb over it and cut into strips measuring 4 × 10 in. (10 × 25 cm). Once set, keep the chocolate strips between two baking sheets to prevent them crinkling.

MAKE THE CHOCOLATE SAUCE

Chop the chocolates into pieces and put them in a mixing bowl. Bring the milk and cream to a boil and pour onto the chocolate, stirring until smooth.

TO ASSEMBLE AND FINISH

Trim the top of each chocolate sponge level with the top of the Flexipan molds. Turn out the sponges and stand them upside down on a baking sheet so the cut sides are at the bottom.

Assemble in reverse order: line the inside of 10 baking rings, 2¾ in. (7 cm) in diameter and 1¾ in. (4.5 cm) deep, with a strip of acetate the same height. Fill them by three-quarters with mousse and then add the sponges. Chill in the refrigerator for 1 hour and then carefully remove the acetate strips. Drain the pears, pat them dry with paper towel and fill the inside of each with pan-fried pear. Place the pears on a wire rack. Melt the glaze to 113°F (45°C) and use to coat the pears. Finally place them on the sponges and surround each with a chocolate band. Serve accompanied with the chocolate sauce.

Recipe photographs, following pages.

MADELEINE
ENTREMETS

In the words of

FRANÇOIS PERRET

The Ritz Paris and *Marcel Proust* are inseparable. The hotel was his second home and the intellectual palace from which he drew his *inspiration*. Therefore, his madeleine, that unforgettable *literary* sleight-of-hand, deserved to have a *patisserie tribute*, dedicated to him by me. For this madeleine, I had fun designing an XXL mold, so that when people saw it, they would be stunned by its *huge size*. But from the first mouthful, its *sensual* curves transport you to another world. But its plump, *rounded* shape is deceptive, as this dessert reveals itself as being as *light* as a feather. It echoes my own 'Proust madeleine': my grandmother's *gâteau mousseline*, my all-time favorite. However, I also wanted this madeleine to have *character*, so I gave it a *bold heart* of chestnut honey, something I particularly like.

Madeleine entremets

I created a special mold for this recipe but here I've adapted the recipe so that you can make it in an 11 in. (28 cm) cake ring, 2 in. (5 cm) deep.

SERVES 8–10

Prep: 1 hr. 30 min.
(rest time not included)
Cook: 30 min.

ALMOND SAVOY SPONGE CAKE
· 1¾ oz. (50 g) slivered almonds
· ⅔ cup (5½ oz./160 g) whole egg
  (about 3 large eggs)
· ¾ cup (5 oz./145 g) superfine sugar
· ⅓ cup (3 oz./80 g) butter
· ¾ cup plus 2 tbsp. (3½ oz./100 g)
  cake flour (type T45)
· ⅓ cup (2 oz./55 g) potato flour
· 1 tsp. (5 g) baking powder

VANILLA IMBIBING SYRUP
· ½ Bourbon vanilla bean
· Generous ¾ cup (200 ml) water
· ⅓ cup (2 oz./60 g) superfine sugar

CARAMEL CRÉMEUX
· 2 sheets (4 g) gelatin
· 3½ cups (820 ml) whipping cream
· 5 oz. (150 g) acacia honey
  (plus a little for the final decoration)
· 7 oz. (190 g) chestnut honey
· 8½ oz. (240 g) glucose syrup
· ¾ cup (7 oz./200 g) egg yolk
  (10 large yolks)

MAKE THE ALMOND SAVOY SPONGE CAKE

Roast the slivered almonds on a baking sheet for 8 minutes in a 300°F (150°C/Gas mark 2) oven. Remove the almonds from the sheet and let them cool. Leave the oven switched on but increase the temperature to 325°F (160°C/Gas mark 3), ventilated setting.

In a stand mixer, whisk the eggs with the sugar. Melt the butter and, while it is still hot, whisk it into the eggs and sugar. Sift the flour, potato flour, and baking powder together, switch off the mixer and fold the dry ingredients into the eggs–butter–sugar mixture with a flexible spatula. Butter and lightly flour an 8½-in. (22-cm) deep straight-sided tart pan. Spread out the roasted almonds over the base in an even layer and then pour over the cake batter so it half-fills the pan. Bake in the oven for 30 minutes. Let cool completely before turning out by running the blade of a knife around the edge between the sides of the pan and the sponge. The sponge needs to be ¾ in. (2 cm) high. If it is higher than this, trim the top using a serrated knife.

MAKE THE VANILLA IMBIBING SYRUP

Slit the vanilla bean lengthwise and scrape out the seeds. Bring the water, sugar, and vanilla to a boil, cover and let infuse for 10 minutes. Allow to cool and then lightly moisten the sponge cake.

MAKE THE CARAMEL CRÉMEUX

Stretch plastic wrap (cling film) over one side of an 8½ in. (22 cm) cake ring and place it on a baking sheet, plastic wrap side down. Soak the gelatin in cold water. Bring the cream to a boil and then take off the heat. In a saucepan, heat both honeys and the glucose to 302°F (150°C), using a thermometer to check the temperature, and then prevent further cook-ing by pouring in the cream. Whisk the egg yolks, add a little of the hot cream mixture, whisking constantly. Add the rest and then pour the entire mixture back into the saucepan and cook, stirring, until it thickens, like a crème anglaise. Add the squeezed out gelatin and strain through a fine-

CRÈME PÂTISSIÈRE
· 1 vanilla bean
· 1¼ cups (300ml) UHT whole milk
· ⅔ tbsp. (10 g) butter
· 3½ tbsp. (1½ oz./40 g) superfine sugar
· 3 tbsp. (1¾ oz./50 g) egg yolk
  (about 2½ large yolks)
· 2 tbsp. (20 g) cornstarch

CHANTILLY MOUSSE
· 1½ sheets (3 g) gelatin
· Scant 3 cups (700 ml) whipping cream
· 7 oz. (200 g) crème pâtissière

GOLD VELVET MIXTURE
· 3½ oz. (100 g) white chocolate
· ⅓ oz. (10 g) Tannea milk chocolate
· 3½ oz. (100 g) cocoa butter
· 1½ tsp. (8 g) metallic gold paste
  or powdered food coloring
· 1 pinch (1 g) liposoluble powdered
  yellow food coloring

CHOCOLATE VELVET MIXTURE
· 3½ oz. (110 g) Carúpano dark
  chocolate, 70% cacao
· 4½ oz. (125 g) cocoa butter
· 1⅓ oz. (40 g) cacao paste

mesh sieve. Do not blend the crémeux but cool it quickly in the freezer and then spread it into the cling wrap-lined cake ring. The crémeux must be exactly ¾ in. (2 cm) high. Freeze it and then lift the sponge cake onto the crémeux, almond side down. Keep chilled.

MAKE THE CRÈME PÂTISSIÈRE
Split the vanilla bean lengthwise and scrape out the seeds. Bring the milk to a boil with the butter, 2½ tsp. (10 g) of the sugar. Whisk the egg yolks with the rest of the sugar until pale and thick, whisk in the cornstarch and then some of the hot milk. Return the mixture to the saucepan and bring to a boil. After 2 minutes boiling, pour onto a baking sheet lined with plastic wrap and cool quickly in the freezer.

MAKE THE CHANTILLY MOUSSE
Soak the gelatin in cold water for 10 minutes. Warm a generous ¾ cup (200 ml) of the whipping cream, add the squeezed-out gelatin and allow to melt. Using a whisk, beat the crème patissière to soften it and make it smooth and then pour it through a fine-mesh sieve into the warm cream and gelatin. Mix and strain through the fine-mesh sieve. When the temperature of the mixture drops to 86°F (30°C), whip the remaining cream and fold in.

MAKE THE GOLD VELVET MIXTURE
Chop the chocolates and the cocoa butter. Add the food colorings and melt everything together in a bain-marie. Strain through a fine-mesh sieve and transfer the mixture to a velvet spray gun. Use at a temperature of 113°F (45°C).

MAKE THE CHOCOLATE VELVET MIXTURE
Chop the chocolate, cocoa butter, and cacao paste. Melt them together in a bain-marie, strain through a fine-mesh sieve and then transfer to a velvet spray gun. Use at a temperature of 113°F (45°C).

TO ASSEMBLE
Fit a band of food-grade acetate, 2 in. (5 cm) wide, around the inside of an 11-in. (28-cm) cake ring, 2 in. (5 cm) deep, placed on a board. Fit the sponge cake in the center, caramel crémeux uppermost, and then pour over the still soft mousse. Spread the top level and then freeze until firm.

Once the entremets is well chilled, remove the ring and the acetate band. First, spray the entremets all over with the gold velvet mixture and then spray it just around the sides with the chocolate velvet mixture, spraying more lightly towards the top to reflect the appearance of a baked madeleine. Finish the decoration with a few drops of honey.

Recipe photographs, following pages.

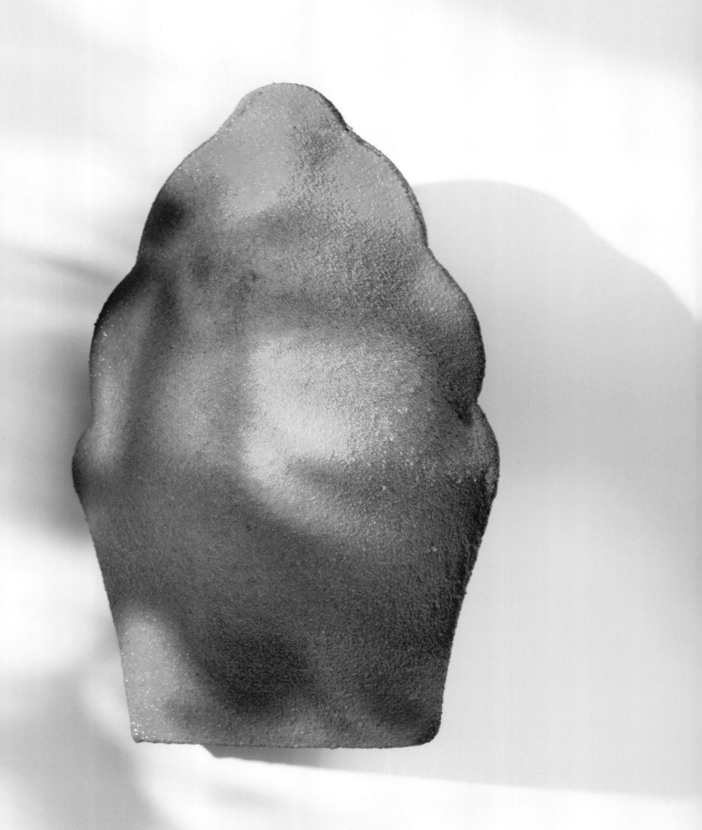

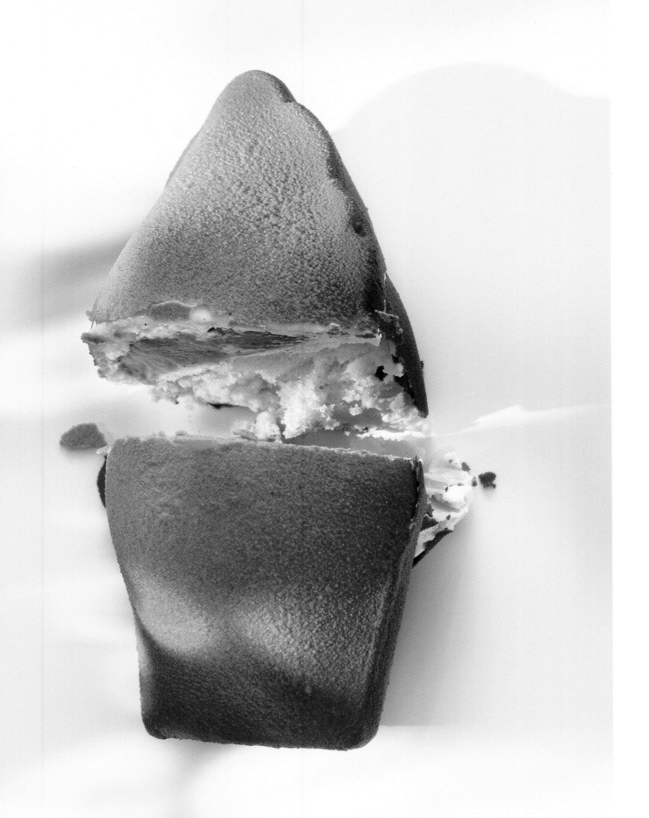

Marbled cake

— entremets —

I created a special mold specifically for this recipe but here I've adapted it so that you can make the cake in a 10¼ in. (26 cm), 2 in. (5 cm) deep, cake ring. You will not need all the chocolate mousse but, because of the amounts of ingredients used, it would be too complicated to make less. You can always put the leftover mousse in the refrigerator and eat it the next day!

SERVES 8

Prep: 1 hr. 30 min. (the crème anglaise needs to be prepared the day before) Cook: 30 min.

IMBIBING SYRUP
· *Generous ¾ cup (200 ml) water*
· *1 oz. (30 g) superfine sugar*

LIGHT SAVOY SPONGE CAKE
· *⅓ cup (3 oz./90 g) butter*
· *¾ cup (6 oz./175 g) eggs (about 4 medium eggs)*
· *Scant 1 cup (5½ oz./160 g) superfine sugar*
· *¾ cup plus 2 tbsp. (4 oz./115 g) cake flour (type T45)*
· *⅓ cup (2 oz./60 g) potato flour*
· *1 tsp. (5 g) baking powder*
· *3 tbsp. (¾ oz./20 g) unsweetened cocoa powder*

VANILLA MOUSSE
· *1 sheet (2 g) gelatin*
· *1½ Bourbon vanilla beans*
· *2 cups (510 ml) crème gastronomique from Étrez, 40% butterfat*
· *⅔ cup (6 oz./170 g) egg yolk (about 8 large yolks)*
· *Scant ⅔ cup (4¼ oz./120 g) superfine sugar*
· *3 tbsp. (45 ml) thick crème fraîche (heavy/double cream)*
· *1½ cups (340 ml) whipping cream, whipped*

MAKE THE IMBIBING SYRUP
Mix the water and sugar together. Bring to a boil and then allow to cool.

MAKE THE LIGHT SAVOY SPONGE CAKE
Preheat the oven to 325°F (170°C/Gas mark 3). Melt the butter. In the bowl of a stand mixer, whisk the eggs with the sugar. When they are thick and mousse-like, add the melted butter. Sift the flour, potato flour, and baking powder together and then fold these into the mixture using a flexible spatula. Divide the mixture in two and fold the cocoa powder into one half using a flexible spatula. Transfer each of the batters to a pastry bag and pipe them into a 9 in. (23 cm) cake ring set on a silicone baking mat, alternating the plain and chocolate batters to give a marbled effect. If necessary, spread the surface level using an angled spatula and then bake for 9–10 minutes in the oven. Allow to cool and then carefully unmold. Imbibe the sponge with the vanilla syrup and then cut it into an 8½ in. (22 cm) round. Keep in the freezer.

MAKE THE VANILLA MOUSSE
The day before, prepare a crème anglaise: soak the gelatin in cold water. Slit the vanilla beans and scrape out the seeds, add to the *crème gastronomique* in a saucepan and bring to a boil. Take off the heat, cover and set aside to infuse. Whisk the egg yolks and the sugar together until they are pale and thick. Slowly pour over the vanilla cream , whisking constantly, and then cook over a low-medium heat until the mixture thickens. Take off the heat and add the squeezed out gelatin sheets. Cover and keep in the refrigerator until the next day and then whip in a stand mixer before adding the thick crème fraiche and, finally, the whipped cream. Transfer to a pastry bag fitted with a smooth tip and keep in the refrigerator.

MAKE THE INTENSE VANILLA FILLING
Snip the vanilla beans into pieces with scissors. Put the milk and vanilla in a Thermomix and cook for 20 minutes at 185°F (85°C), speed 3. If you do not have a Thermomix, cook in a saucepan at a gentle simmer (so the surface is just trembling) for 20 minutes and then process in a blender.

INTENSE VANILLA FILLING
· 4½ Bourbon vanilla beans
· ⅔ cup (150 ml) whole milk,
  plus a little for completion
· 7 oz. (195 g) glucose syrup
· Scant 1 cup (225 ml) whipping
  cream from Étrez

CHOCOLATE MOUSSE FOR MARBLING
· 4½ oz. (125 g) Sambirano dark chocolate
· ½ cup (125 ml) whipping cream
· 2 sheets (4 g) gelatin
· ⅓ cup (3 oz./80 g) egg yolk
  (about 4 large yolks) and 1¼ tbsp
  (15 g) superfine sugar
· ½ cup (4¼ oz./120 g) egg white
  (about 4 large whites) and 2½ tsp.
  (10 g) superfine sugar

CHOCOLATE VELVET MIXTURE
· 3½ oz. (100 g) cocoa butter
· 2 oz. (50 g) Carúpano dark chocolate,
  70% cacao solids

At the end of the cooking time, blend for 1 minute. Strain through a fine-mesh sieve, pressing down vigorously on the mixture with the bowl of a small ladle so as to extract the maximum flavor. Top up with extra milk to bring the quantity back to the original ⅔ cup (150 ml).

In a small saucepan, and using an instant-read thermometer, cook the glucose syrup to 266°F (130°C) and then prevent further cooking by adding the infused vanilla milk and whipping cream. Cook until the mixture thickens slightly. Spread it over the frozen sponge and put back in the freezer.

MAKE THE CHOCOLATE MOUSSE FOR MARBLING
Melt the chocolate in a bain-marie to 122°F (50°C). In a stand mixer, whip the cream lightly to very soft peaks, taking care not to overwhip it. Keep in the refrigerator. Soak the gelatin in cold water for 10 minutes, squeeze excess water from the sheets, and then melt them in a bowl in the microwave.

Whisk the egg yolks in the stand mixer with the 1¼ tbsp. (15 g) of sugar until they are pale and mousse-like (to a sabayon), and then fold in the melted gelatin. At the same time, whisk the egg whites to soft peaks, stiffening them by whisking in the 2½ tsp. (10 g) sugar. Fold in the melted chocolate and then straightaway fold half the egg whites and half the sabayon together. Begin by mixing with a whisk and then add the rest of the whites and the sabayon using a flexible spatula to incorporate them. Keep in the refrigerator.

MAKE THE CHOCOLATE VELVET MIXTURE
Melt the ingredients for the chocolate velvet mixture in a bain-marie and then strain through a fine-mesh sieve. Pour into a velvet spray gun and use at 113°F (45°C).

TO ASSEMBLE
Remember that the sponge and the intense vanilla filling must previously have been assembled and frozen. Spoon the chocolate mousse into a pastry bag fitted with a plain tip. Place a sheet of food-grade acetate on a baking sheet, line the sides of a 10¼ in. (26 cm) cake ring, 2 in. (5 cm) deep, with a strip of acetate and place the ring on the acetate sheet. Pipe lines of chocolate mousse in irregular patterns into the ring and then put the whole thing in the freezer. When the dessert is well-chilled, pipe the vanilla mousse into the spaces between the lines of chocolate mousse. Fill the ring three-quarters full with the vanilla mousse and place the sponge with the vanilla filling in the center, smoothing the top level. Freeze until completely solid. To add the finishing touches, the assembled dessert must be frozen. Unmold it and, using the spray gun, spray the underneath of the dessert with chocolate velvet mixture, and then the top.

Recipe photographs, previous pages.

All-vanilla entremets

SERVES 8–10

Prep: 1 hr. 30 min.
Cook: 55 min.

VANILLA MOUSSE
· 1 Bourbon vanilla bean
· Generous ¾ cup (200 ml)
  whipping cream, 33% butterfat
· 1½ sheets (3 g) gelatin
· 3 egg yolks
· ⅓ cup (2¼ oz./65 g) superfine sugar
· Generous ¾ cup (200 ml)
  whipping cream, whipped

IMBIBING SYRUP
· ½ vanilla bean
· 2 tbsp. (1 oz./25 g) sugar
· Scant ½ cup (100 ml) water

SAVOY SPONGE CAKE
· ⅖ cup (2 oz./55 g) cake flour
  (type T45)
· 2½ tbsp. (1 oz./25 g) potato flour
· ½ tsp. (2 g) baking powder
· 3 tbsp. (1½ oz./45 g) butter
· ⅓ cup (2½ oz./75 g) superfine sugar
· 1 large whole egg plus 1 egg yolk

MAKE THE VANILLA MOUSSE

Slit the vanilla bean lengthwise, scrape out the seeds and cut it into small pieces. In a saucepan, bring the cream to a boil with the vanilla bean and seeds. Take the saucepan off the heat, cover, and let infuse for 15 minutes. Soak the gelatin in cold water.

Whisk the egg yolks and sugar together until pale and thick. Add the hot cream, a little at a time, whisking constantly, pour back into the saucepan and cook over low heat, stirring with a spatula. When the cream thickens, take it off the heat and process with an immersion blender. Strain through a fine-mesh sieve and add the squeezed-out gelatin sheets. Let cool completely and then fold in the whipped cream. Pour the mousse into an 8 in. (20 cm) cake ring on a silicone baking mat, and chill in the refrigerator .

MAKE THE IMBIBING SYRUP

Slit the half vanilla bean lengthwise and scrape out the seeds. Add it to the sugar and water in a saucepan and bring to a boil. Cover and let infuse. Use hot.

MAKE THE SAVOY SPONGE CAKE

Preheat the oven to 325°F (160°C/Gas mark 3). Sift the flour with the potato flour and baking powder. Melt the butter. Whisk the sugar and eggs in a stand mixer, add the hot melted butter and then fold in the dry ingredients with a flexible spatula. Pour the batter into a 7 in. (18 cm) cake ring set on a silicone baking mat placed on a baking sheet. Bake for 8–10 minutes (according to your oven). Trim the top of the sponge evenly so it is 1¼ in. (3 cm) high. Using a brush, moisten with the syrup and then freeze until firm.

CRÈME BRÛLÉE FILLING

- *½ sheet (1 g) gelatin*
- *1 Bourbon vanilla bean*
- *3½ tbsp. (50 ml) milk*
- *½ cup (130 ml) whipping or heavy (double) cream*
- *2 egg yolks*
- *2 tbsp. (1 oz./25 g) superfine sugar*

VANILLA ICING

- *3 sheets (6 g) gelatin*
- *¼ cup (2½ oz./70 g) unsweetened condensed milk*
- *3½ oz. (100 g) white chocolate, chopped*
- *Vanilla powder*
- *3½ tbsp. (50 ml) water*
- *½ cup (3½ oz./100 g) superfine sugar*
- *3½ oz. (100 g) glucose syrup.*

MAKE THE CRÈME BRÛLÉE FILLING

Preheat the oven to 190°F (90°C/Gas on lowest setting). Soak the gelatin in cold water for 10 minutes.

Slit the vanilla bean lengthwise and scrape out the seeds. Bring the milk and cream to a boil with the vanilla bean and seeds, take off the heat, cover and let infuse for 10 minutes. Add the squeezed out gelatin.

Whisk the egg yolks with the sugar until pale and thick. Strain the hot cream mixture through a fine-mesh sieve onto the whisked yolks and sugar, whisking lightly.

Stretch plastic wrap (cling film), suitable for use in an oven, over one side of a 7-in. (18-cm) cake ring. Place the ring on a baking sheet, plastic wrap down, and pour in the mixture, which must reach ⅓ in. (1 cm) up the sides of the ring. Cook in the oven for 45 minutes and then allow to cool.

MAKE THE VANILLA ICING

Soak the gelatin in cold water for about 10 minutes. Place the condensed milk, white chocolate, and vanilla powder in a mixing bowl.
Heat the water, sugar, and syrup to 217°F (103°C), using a thermometer to check the temperature. Pour onto the milk, chocolate, and vanilla powder and add the squeezed-out gelatin. Process with an immersion blender, taking care not to incorporate air into the mixture. When ready to use the icing, heat it to between 86 and 95°F (30-35°C).

TO ASSEMBLE

Fold the whipped cream into the custard. The entremets is assembled by layering the individual elements in reverse order in an 8 in. (20 cm) cake ring with plastic wrap stretched over one side of the ring. Place the ring, with the plastic wrap downwards, and then begin the assembly. First of all, pour the mousse into the ring . Take the sponge cake out of the freezer and place the crème brûlée filling on the trimmed side. Turn the sponge over and place it in the center of the mousse, with the crème brûlée filling downwards. The top of the sponge and the crème must be level with the top of the ring. Smooth the surface using a spatula and put in the freezer. Once the entremets is well-chilled, unmold and ice it.

Recipe photographs, following pages.

Chocolate truffle tart

SERVES 8–10

Prep: 1 hr. 30 min.
*Rest: 30 min. (prepare the pastry
the day before)*
Cook: 25 min.

**GLUTEN-FREE CHOCOLATE
SHORTBREAD PASTRY**
- *1 cup (5 oz./150 g) rice flour*
- *¾ cup plus 1 tbsp. (3½ oz./100 g)
  cornstarch*
- *6 tbsp. (1½ oz./40 g) unsweetened
  cocoa powder*
- *1 cup (7¾ oz./220 g) butter, softened*
- *¾ cup (3½ oz./100 g) confectioners' sugar*
- *½ tsp. (2 g) salt*
- *3 tbsp. (1½ oz./40 g) egg white
  (about 1 large white)*

CACAO NIBS CREAM
- *¼ cup (2 oz./60 g) butter, softened*
- *⅓ cup (2 oz./60 g) superfine sugar*
- *4 tbsp. (2 oz./60 g) egg
  (about 1 large egg) at room temperature*
- *2 oz. (60 g) cacao nibs*

CRÈME PÂTISSIÈRE
- *1 vanilla bean*
- *1¼ cups (300 ml) UHT whole milk*
- *1 tbsp. (½ oz./10 g) butter*
- *3¼ tbsp. (1½ oz./40 g) superfine sugar*
- *2 tbsp. (1¾ oz./50 g) egg yolk
  (about 3 medium yolks)*
- *3 tbsp. (¾ oz./20 g) cornstarch*

MAKE THE GLUTEN-FREE CHOCOLATE SHORTBREAD PASTRY
The day before, sift together the rice flour, cornstarch, and cocoa powder. In a stand mixer, beat the butter until soft and creamy, add the confectioners' sugar and salt. Add the egg white and then fold in the sifted dry ingredients. Roll out the pastry ¹⁄₁₆ in. (2 mm) thick, lift it onto a baking sheet and let rest in the refrigerator. The next day, preheat the oven to 325°F (170°C/Gas mark 3). Cut the pastry into an 11 in. (28 cm) round and then divide this into 8 or 10 triangles, without separating them. Place between two black silicone baking mats and bake in the oven for 12 minutes.

MAKE THE CACAO NIBS CREAM
Beat the softened butter and sugar together until light and creamy. Be careful not to let the butter become 'grainy': use a gas gun to warm it, if necessary. Add the egg, and then the cacao nibs. Take care not to emulsify the cream.

MAKE THE CRÈME PÂTISSIÈRE
Slit the vanilla bean lengthwise and scrape out the seeds. In a saucepan, bring the milk to a boil with the butter and 2½ tsp. (10 g) of the sugar. Whisk the egg yolks with the rest of the sugar to soft peaks, add the cornstarch and then some of the hot milk. Pour the mixture back into the saucepan, stir to combine everything, and bring to a boil. After boiling for 2 minutes, pour onto a baking sheet lined with plastic wrap, press another sheet over the top, and cool quickly in the freezer.

MAKE THE FRANGIPANE CREAM WITH CACAO NIBS
Beat the crème pâtissière to loosen it and add the cacao nibs cream. Spread the frangipane into a 10¼ in. (26 cm) round on a baking sheet and cook it for about 10 minutes in a 325°F (170°C/Gas mark 3) oven. Watch carefully to ensure it only colors lightly.

FRANGIPANE CREAM WITH CACAO NIBS
· *2⅝ oz (75 g) crème pâtissière*
· *8 oz. (225 g) cacao nibs cream*

CHOCOLATE GANACHE
· *6⅓ oz. (180 g) Samana chocolate, 62% cacao*
· *2⅓ oz. (65 g) Tannea chocolate, 42% cacao*
· *1 sheet (2 g) gelatin*
· *½ cup (120 ml) UHT whipping cream*
· *½ cup (120 ml) milk*
· *¾ oz. (20 g) invert sugar (trimoline)*
· *2 tbsp. (1 oz./25 g) butter*
· *1 tbsp. (¾ oz./20 g) egg yolk (about 1 large yolk)*
· *½ cup (120 ml) whipping cream*

CHANTILLY CREAM WITH COCOA
· *2½ cups (600 ml) UHT whipping cream*
· *½ cup (2 oz./60 g) confectioners' sugar, sifted*
· *4 tbsp. (1 oz./30 g) unsweetened cocoa powder, sifted*

TO FINISH
· *Confectioners' sugar*
· *Unsweetened cocoa powder*

MAKE THE CHOCOLATE GANACHE

Break the chocolates into small pieces and put them in a bowl. Soak the gelatin in cold water.

Bring the UHT cream, milk, invert sugar (trimoline), and butter to a boil. Remove from the heat and let cool sufficiently until you can add the egg yolk without it scrambling. Heat the mixture to 185°F (85°C). Strain through a fine-mesh sieve onto the chocolates, add the squeezed out gelatin sheet, and process with an immersion blender. Allow the temperature to reduce down again. During this time, whip the cream to soft peaks. When the temperature of the ganache reaches 104°F (40°C) or less, fold in the whipped cream with a flexible spatula.

Pour half the ganache into a tart ring, 10¼ in. (26 cm) in diameter and ¾ in. (2 cm) deep, so the ganache comes halfway up the sides of the ring. Top with the frangipane, chill for 30 minutes, and then add the rest of the ganache. Leave to harden in the freezer, cut into 8 or 10 triangles, and return it to the freezer.

MAKE THE CHANTILLY CREAM WITH COCOA

In a stand mixer, whisk all the ingredients without letting the cream stiffen too much.

TO FINISH

Dip the frozen triangles of ganache–frangipane into the Chantilly cream, spearing each one at the back with the point of a small knife. Lift them out of the cream, without neatening the tops, but smooth the edges with a small spatula. Dust the top and underside generously with confectioners' sugar and then dust with the cocoa powder in the same way. Repeat with the remaining triangles and place each one on a pastry base.

Recipe photograph, following page.

181

Mont Blanc tart

Take care to ensure that the appearance of the assembled "mountain" is exactly right: the meringues must be aligned and their different sizes clearly visible.

SERVES 10

Prep: 1 hr. 30 min.
Cook: 2 hr. 30 min.

SAVOY SPONGE CAKE
· 3 tbsp. (1½ oz./45 g) butter
· ⅓ cup (3 oz./80 g) superfine sugar
· 6 tbsp. (3 oz./90 g) eggs
  (about 2 medium eggs)
· ½ cup (2 oz./55 g) cake flour (type T45)
· 2½ tbsp. (1 oz./30 g) potato flour
· ½ tsp. (2 g) baking powder

MERINGUE
· ⅔ cup (5 oz./150 g) egg white
  (about 5 large whites)
· 1 cup plus 1 tbsp. (8 oz./225 g)
  superfine sugar

CRÈME PÂTISSIÈRE
· 1 vanilla bean
· 1¼ cups (300 ml) UHT whole milk
· 1 tbsp. (½ oz./10 g) butter
· 3¼ tbsp. (1½ oz./40 g) superfine sugar
· 2 tbsp. (2 oz./50 g) egg yolk
  (about 3 medium yolks)
· 3 tbsp. (¾ oz./20 g) cornstarch

EXTRA RICH CREAM
· 1½ sheets (3 g) gelatin
· 1 cup (250 ml) whipping cream
· 1 tbsp. (½ oz./15 g) confectioners' sugar
· 1 oz. (25 g) mascarpone
· 2½ oz. (70 g) crème pâtissière

MAKE THE SAVOY SPONGE CAKE
Preheat the oven to 325°F (165°C/Gas mark 3). Melt the butter. In the bowl of a stand mixer, beat the sugar with the eggs. When thick and mousse-like, add the melted butter. Sift the flour, potato flour, and baking powder together, and fold in using a flexible spatula. Spread out in a ¼ in. (5 mm) layer onto a baking sheet lined with parchment paper. Bake in the oven for 7 minutes and then cut out 10 disks using a pastry cutter, 2 in. (5 cm) in diameter.

MAKE THE MERINGUE
Preheat the oven to 225°F (110°C/Gas mark ¼). Whisk the egg whites with the sugar in a stand mixer to stiff peaks. Heat them briefly with a gas gun and then spoon the meringue into a pastry bag. Pipe large peaks onto a silicone baking sheet in three different diameters: 1⅜ in. (3.5 cm), 1¾ in. (4.5 cm), and 2¼ in. (5.5 cm), 10 of each size. Cook for 2 hours in the oven and then let the meringues cool. Hollow the bases out with a plain piping tip and store them, in their groups of three, in a dry place.

MAKE THE CRÈME PÂTISSIÈRE
Slit the vanilla bean lengthwise and scrape out the seeds. In a saucepan, bring the milk and butter to a boil with 2½ tsp. (10 g) of the sugar and the vanilla bean and seeds. Remove from the heat and cover. Whisk the egg yolks with the remaining sugar until they are pale and thick, add the cornstarch, pour over some of the milk , whisking constantly, and then pour the mixture back into the saucepan. Let boil for 2 minutes, pour onto a baking sheet, cover with a sheet of plastic wrap (cling film) and cool quickly in the freezer.

MAKE THE EXTRA RICH CREAM
Soak the gelatin in cold water for 10 minutes, squeeze out the sheets and dissolve in a bowl in a microwave. Using an immersion blender, process together the whipping cream, confectioners' sugar, and mascarpone, before whisking them lightly in a stand mixer. Transfer this mixture to another bowl, wash and dry the stand mixer bowl, and beat the crème pâtissière in it to soften it. Add the dissolved gelatin, mix well, and whisk in one-third of the mascarpone mixture, mixing again very gently. Fold in the rest of the mascarpone mixture using a flexible spatula.

SWEET SHORTCRUST PASTRY

· ½ vanilla bean
· ⅔ cup (5¼ oz./150 g) butter, softened,
  plus a little to grease the ring
· ⅔ cup (3 oz./90 g) confectioners' sugar
· ⅓ cup (1 oz./30 g) ground almonds
· 1 egg
· 1 pinch (1 g) fleur de sel
· 2 cups (9 oz./250 g) all-purpose flour
· 1 egg yolk beaten with a few drops
  of water for glazing

CHESTNUT CREAM FILLING

· 1½ oz. (40 g) unsweetened condensed milk
· 8 oz. (225 g) chestnut spread (purée)
· 9 oz. (240 g) chestnut paste
· 1 tsp. (5 ml) dark rum

TO ASSEMBLE

· Dark rum
· Confectioners' sugar
· Generous ¾ cup (200 ml)
  crème gastronomique *from Étrez*

MAKE THE SWEET SHORTCRUST PASTRY

Slit the vanilla bean lengthwise and scrape out the seeds. You only use the seeds for this step. Using an electric beater, whisk the softened butter with the confectioners' sugar and ground almonds. Add the egg, fleur de sel, and vanilla seeds. Sift the flour and fold it in gently to make a smooth dough. Wrap in plastic wrap (cling film) and let rest in the refrigerator for 1 hour.

Preheat the oven to 325°F (160°C/Gas mark 3). Using a rolling pin, roll out the dough ¹⁄₁₆ in. (2 mm) thick and line it into 10 tartlet molds, 2¾ in. (7 cm) in diameter. Place on a silicone baking mat and bake in the oven for 20 minutes. Take the tartlets out of the oven and brush the insides with the egg and water mixture to glaze and seal them. Return the tartlets to the oven for 1 minute. Let cool.

CHESTNUT CREAM FILLING

Mix together the ingredients for the chestnut cream filling.

TO ASSEMBLE

Lightly brush the Clément® rum over both sides of the Savoy sponge disks. Spread a thin layer of extra rich cream into each tartlet case and place the imbibed sponge disks on top. Add the cream and smooth the tops flat with a spatula.

Keeping the meringues in their groups of three, fill the largest meringues with chestnut cream, place them in the tartlets and dust with confectioners' sugar. Fill the middle-sized meringues with the extra rich cream and the smallest with chestnut cream. Place the middle-sized and smallest meringues on a sheet of parchment paper and dust them with confectioners' sugar before placing on top of the largest meringues. Serve with a little *crème gastronomique*.

Recipe photograph, page 183.

— *Light-as-air* —
Lemon meringue tart

SERVES 10

Prep: 1 hr.
Rest: 1 hr.
Cook: 30 min.

SWEET SHORTCRUST PASTRY
· ⅔ cup (5 oz./150 g) butter, softened,
  plus a little for the ring
· ⅔ cup (3 oz./90 g) confectioners' sugar
· ⅓ cup (1 oz./30 g) ground almonds
· 1 egg
· 1 pinch (1 g) fleur de sel
· ½ vanilla bean (only the seeds)
· 2 cups (9 oz./250 g) all-purpose flour

LEMON CREAM
· ¾ cup (185 ml) lemon juice
· Zest of 2 lemons, removed in strips using
  a vegetable peeler or a Microplane® grater
· 1 cup (6½ oz./184 g) superfine sugar
· ¾ cup (6 oz./170 g) eggs
  (about 4 medium eggs)
· Generous 1 cup (9 oz./260 g) butter,
  diced

ALMOND CREAM WITH LEMON
· ½ egg
· Scant ¼ cup (1½ oz./40 g) superfine sugar
· ½ cup (1½ oz./40 g) ground almonds
· 3 oz. (90 g) lemon cream

LEMON BLANCMANGE
· 1 sheet (2 g) gelatin
· ⅔ cup (5¼ oz./150 g) fresh egg white
  (about 5 large whites)
· ½ cup (4 oz./110 g) superfine sugar
· Oil to grease the rings and
  the baking sheet

MAKE THE SWEET SHORTCRUST PASTRY

Mix the softened butter with the confectioners' sugar and ground almonds. Add the egg, fleur de sel, and vanilla seeds. Sift the flour and gently work it into the other ingredients until evenly incorporated. Gather the dough into a ball, wrap it in plastic wrap (cling film) and let rest in the refrigerator for 1 hour.

Preheat the oven to 325°F (160°C/Gas mark 3). Roll out the pastry ¹⁄₁₆ in. (2 mm) thick and use it to line an 8½ in. (22 cm) pastry ring. Bake in the oven for 20 minutes. After the pastry is cooked, leave the oven switched on.

MAKE THE LEMON CREAM

In a saucepan, heat the lemon juice and zests with half the sugar. Whisk the eggs with the rest of the sugar until pale and thick and then whisk in the hot juice and zests. Cook, stirring constantly, as for a crème pâtissière, letting the mixture boil for 3 minutes. Strain it through a fine-mesh sieve onto the butter and then process with an immersion blender. Part of this cream will be mixed with the almond cream, the rest will fill the tart and the hollows in the blancmange layer.

MAKE THE ALMOND CREAM WITH LEMON

Whisk the egg and sugar together until pale and thick. Incorporate the ground almonds and lemon cream. Spoon this cream into a pastry bag and pipe it over the pre-baked pastry. Put the pastry back in the oven at 325°F (160°C/Gas mark 3) and cook for 4 minutes.

MAKE THE LEMON BLANCMANGE

Soak the gelatin in cold water, squeeze out the excess water and dissolve in a bowl in a micro-wave. In the bowl of a stand mixer fitted with the whisk attachment, gently whisk the egg whites with the sugar to soft peaks. Strain the gelatin and then fold it into the whisked egg whites until evenly incorporated. Spoon the mixture into a pastry bag. With a small piece of oiled parchment paper, grease 10 baking rings, 3 in. (8 cm) in diameter and ¾ in. (1.5 cm) deep, and put them on a baking sheet that has also been greased with oil.

Pipe the mixture into the rings, filling the rings and smoothing the tops level with an angled spatula. Cook in a steam oven at 176°F (80°C) for 3 minutes. If you do not have a steam oven, microwave on full power for about 15–20 seconds, no longer. At the end of the cooking time, remove the rings. Let cool. Using round cookie cutters in three different sizes, 1 in. (2.5 cm), ⅗ in. (1.5 cm), and ¾ in. (2 cm), press several hollows in the top of each.

TO ASSEMBLE

Fill the tart with lemon cream over the layer of almond–lemon cream and smooth the surface with a spatula. Arrange the blancmange over the cream and then fill the hollows with the rest of the lemon cream.

Mellow raspberry
— *tablet* —

SERVES 8–10
Prep: 40 min.
Rest: about 1 hr.
Cook: 6 min.

SAVOY SPONGE CAKE
· *3 tbsp. (1½ oz./40 g) butter*
· *⅓ cup (2½ oz./45 g) cake flour (type T45)*
· *2 tbsp. (¾ oz./20 g) potato flour*
· *¾ tsp. (3 g) baking powder*
· *⅓ cup (2½ oz./70 g) eggs
  (about 2 medium eggs)*
· *⅓ cup (2½ oz./70 g) superfine sugar*

RASPBERRY PASTE
· *7 oz. (190 g) raspberry purée*
· *5 tsp. (20 g) superfine sugar mixed
  with 1 tsp. (4 g) yellow pectin*
· *1 cup (7 oz./200 g) superfine sugar*
· *2 oz. (50 g) glucose syrup*
· *Scant ½ cup (100 ml) raspberry
  eau-de-vie mixed with ¾ tsp. (3 g)
  citric acid*

TO FINISH
· *9 oz, (250 g) Carúpano chocolate,
  70% cacao*

MAKE THE SAVOY SPONGE CAKE

Preheat the oven to 325°F (165°C/Gas mark 3), ventilated setting. Melt the butter and keep it hot. Sift the flour with the potato flour and baking powder.

In the bowl of a stand mixer, whisk the eggs with the sugar until pale and mousse-like. Add the hot butter and then switch off the mixer. Fold the sifted flour mixture into the whisked eggs and sugar using a flexible spatula.

Spread the batter in an even layer into a 9 in. (23 cm) square baking frame set on a silicone baking mat and bake in the oven for 6 minutes. Remove the frame as soon as the sponge comes out of the oven and place a perforated baking sheet on top, pressing down on it lightly to flatten the sponge.

MAKE THE RASPBERRY PASTE

Lightly oil the inside of a 9 in. (23 cm.) square baking frame and place it on a silicone baking mat.

Using an instant-read thermometer, heat the raspberry purée to 140°F (60°C). Stir in the sugar and pectin mixture and bring to a boil. Add the 1 cup (7 oz./200 g) sugar and glucose syrup. Cook until the temperature reaches 226°F (108°C) and then add the raspberry eau-de-vie and citric acid mixture. Allow to stand briefly until the bubbles in the mixture have dispersed before pouring the mixture into the baking frame.

TO FINISH

Pour the raspberry paste into the baking frame and immediately sit the sponge on top. Exert a light pressure when doing this so that the two layers adhere firmly together. Let cool completely.

Temper the chocolate by melting it in a bowl in a bain-marie until the temperature reaches 122°F (50°C) on an instant-read thermometer. Remove the chocolate from the bain-marie and dip the base of the bowl into a bowl of cold water so the overall temperature of the chocolate drops rapidly to 81°F (27°C) and not just at the bottom. Return the chocolate to the bain-marie to liquify it, reheating it to a maximum of 88°F–90°F (31°C–32°C). Maintain the chocolate at this temperature without heating it any further.

Turn the baking frame over and, using a pastry brush, brush the base of the sponge with the tempered chocolate. Cut into 2½ × 4½ in. (6 × 11 cm) rectangles and dip them in the tempered chocolate. Let set on a wire rack.

My personal
favorite

I never tire of this light, *melt-in-the-mouth* cake. It's a really simple dessert, but is so good. For me it represents 100% of everything a patisserie should be. You can *eat it at any time of day*, from breakfast until dinner, not forgetting afternoon tea. It can be eaten on its own or accompanied with crème anglaise, and anywhere you choose: on fine china plates at a *very chic tea party*, on a corner of the kitchen table with friends, on a checked tablecloth at a family picnic... It's *the ultimate cake to share*. And it travels and keeps well. It will cross oceans in your luggage, following you everywhere you go. It is the *comfort blanket* you carry with you. A small thing that is guaranteed to make *everyone happy*. And you too, I hope.

My personal favorite

Marbled cake

The quantities given are for making two cakes but I would recommend you follow them as the ingredients will be easier to weigh out.

SERVES 8–10.

Prep: 30 min.
Cook: 1hr. 30min.

VANILLA CAKE MIXTURE
- ¾ cup plus 3 tbsp. (3½ oz./110 g) all-purpose flour
- ¾ tsp. (3 g) baking powder
- ¼ cup (2¼ oz./60 g) butter, softened, a little for the cake pans, plus scant
- ¼ cup (1¾ oz./50 g) for when baking the cakes
- ¾ cup (5¼ oz./150 g) superfine sugar
- ½ tsp. (2 g) vanilla powder
- ½ tsp. (2 g) fleur de sel
- 1 egg
- Scant ½ cup (100 ml) whipping cream

COCOA CAKE MIXTURE
- ¾ cup plus 2 tbsp. (3½ oz./100 g) all-purpose flour
- ¾ tsp. (3 g) baking powder
- ¼ cup (2¼ oz./60 g) butter, softened
- ¾ cup (5¼ oz./150 g) superfine sugar
- 1 egg
- 3 tbsp. (¾ oz./20 g) unsweetened cocoa powder
- Scant ½ cup (100 ml) whipping cream

IMBIBING SYRUP
- 1 cup (250 ml) water
- ¼ cup (1¾ oz./50 g) superfine sugar
- 1 tbsp. (15 ml) dark rum

ICING
- 1 lb. 10 oz. (750 g) brown compound coating
- 9 oz. (250 g) Carúpano bittersweet chocolate, 70% cacao, chopped
- ½ cup (125 ml) grape seed oil

MAKE THE VANILLA CAKE MIXTURE
Butter two loaf pans, 9½–10¼ in. (24–26 cm) long.

Sift the flour and baking powder together.

In the bowl of a stand mixer, beat together the ¼ cup (2¼ oz./60 g) butter, sugar, vanilla powder, and salt. Without switching off the motor, add the egg. Switch the motor off and fold the ingredients together (using a bowl scraper or flexible spatula, scrape the sides of the bowl to bring the mixture around the edges to the center). Restart the motor and incorporate the sifted flour and baking powder, and finally the cream. Ensure the batter is smooth and evenly mixed but don't have the motor running for too long. Spoon the batter into a disposable plastic pastry bag and keep it chilled.

MAKE THE COCOA CAKE MIXTURE
Sift the flour and baking powder together.

In the bowl of a stand mixer, beat together the butter, sugar, and salt. Without switching off the motor, add the egg. Switch the motor off and fold the ingredients together (using a bowl scraper or flexible spatula, scrape the sides of the bowl to bring the mixture sticking to the edges to the center). Restart the motor and incorporate the sifted flour and baking powder, then the cocoa powder, and finally the cream. Ensure the batter is smooth and evenly mixed but don't have the motor running for too long. Spoon the batter into a disposable plastic pastry bag.

Spoon the scant ¼ cup (1¾ oz./50 g) softened butter into another pastry bag or paper piping cone to use before baking the cakes.

TO BAKE AND ICE
Preheat the oven to 275°F (145°C/Gas mark 1).

Snip the points off the pastry bags filled with the vanilla and chocolate cake mixtures, and pipe the mixtures alternately into the cake pans to create a marbled effect. When the pans are full, pipe a line of butter lengthwise down the center of each cake. Bake in the oven for 1 hour 30 minutes.

Meanwhile, make the imbibing syrup by bringing the water and sugar to a boil. Remove from the heat and add the rum.

Unmold the cakes when they come out of the oven, stand them on a wire rack over a baking sheet, and spoon over the hot imbibing syrup. Let the cakes cool and then put them in the freezer so they can be iced more easily.

Melt the ingredients for the icing together in a bain-marie to 113°F (45°C). Process with an immersion blender, strain through a fine-mesh sieve, and then use to ice the still-frozen cakes.

Allow the cakes to come to room temperature.

"*A dessert must arouse desire,
its deliciousness must make you
want to come back for more.*"

François Perret

**FIRST
PLEASURES
OF THE DAY**
— 16 —

**AFTERNOON
TEA REGAINED**
— 64 —

Brioche French toast	18
Fresh fruit muesli	20
Waffles	22
Hot chocolate	24
Brioche	28
Toasted brioche with butter and mirabelles	30
My sweet Bressane tart	34
Citrus "flower show" with Suzette sauce	36

Teddy bear marshmallows	66
Honey madeleines	70
Vanilla chouquettes	72
Raspberry gateau	74
Florentines	76
Chocolate soufflé meringues	78
My mother's fig tart	82
Grated fennel, vinaigrette, and lemon sorbet	86
Tart with blackberries and celery	90
Green asparagus & genmaicha green tea	92
Hazelnut meringue, aged parmesan, and lemon sauce	96

**IN THE
COURSE OF
A LUNCH**
— 38 —

Zacapa rum baba with whipped Étrez cream	40
Cherry tarte Tatin with Étrez cream	46
Tarte Tatin	50
Crisp meringue with melting Carúpano chocolate	54
Flourless chocolate cake with crème anglaise	60
Rhubarb with herbs, yogurt, and pink peppercorns	62

GRAND EVENING DESSERTS
— 98 —

Rhubarb	100
Meyer lemon	104
Wild blueberry crackers	108
Wild blackberries with meringue and whipped cream	110

Crème caramel — 114
Caramel and milk mousse
Meringue with crisp, golden almonds
Cigarette russe

Strawberry — 118
Conserve, burrata, olive oil, and vinegar
Ciflorette strawberries, cream from Bresse, and brown sugar
Toasted brioche

Jamaya chocolate — 122
Meringue Concorde, raspberry granita
Iced parfait enclosed in curls, pepper, and salt
Raspberries

Honey — 126
Faisselle, honeyed red onion jam
Honeycomb
Chocolate alveoli

Quince — 130
Dim sum
Poached quince, crystallized walnuts, mint, and whipped cream
Quince jelly

FEASTS GREAT AND SMALL AROUND THE CLOCK
— 134 —

Little hazelnut boats	138
Little caramel boats	140
Vanilla crème brûlée	144
Vanilla meringue	148
Pomelo cheesecake	150
The floating island that does not float	154
Raspberry Charlotte	160
Pear in a cage	162
Madeleine entremets	168
Marbled cake entremets	172
All-vanilla entremets	176
Chocolate truffle tart	180
Mont Blanc tart	184
Light-as-air lemon meringue tart	186
Mellow raspberry tablet	188

MY PERSONAL FAVORITE — **190**

Marbled cake	192

At the heart of the French capital on the Place Vendôme, the Ritz Paris possesses a charm that is impossible to define but which makes it one of the most legendary hotels in the world.

Thank you to this prestigious establishment and to my colleagues who every day inspire our work. Without you, our cakes would certainly not taste the same.

Thank you to my incomparable team for their invaluable support in the creation of this book: Silvia Vigneux, who has worked alongside me for many years, Adeline Robinault, Clément Tilly, Julien Loubere, Stéphane Ollivier...

Thank you to Christophe Messina, Matthieu Carlin, Julien Merceron and many others, whose precious advice has allowed me to move forward and develop my own style.

Thank you,
To the Executive Management of the Ritz Paris,
To Éditions de La Martinière, the publishers who made this book possible,
To Bernhard Winkelmann who captured all the delicacy of my desserts in his photos,
To Sophie Brissaud for editing the recipes,
To Marie-Catherine de la Roche and her unique pen,
To Michel Troisgros for adding his name to the foreword of this book,
To Nicolas Sale for our daily collaboration within the hotel,
To the pastry chefs and cooks I have worked alongside who gave me the chance to learn and to grow,
To our suppliers who always think of us and are very attentive to our needs.

And, of course, to my family, my parents, and my paternal grandparents. To Aurélie, my partner, and my two children Cléo and Tom, who support me more than ever in my life as a pastry chef.

And, obviously, thank you to all the lovers of great food without whom my work would count for nothing. It is because of you and for you alone that I put such passion into my job.

See you very soon at the Ritz Paris,

François Perret

Graphic design and production: Laurence Maillet

Photographs: Bernhard Winkelmann
Set dressing (p.38, 64, 134): Nathalie Nannini

Photograph (p.11): Vincent Leroux

Publishing: Virginie Mahieux assisted by Pauline Dubuisson

Texts (p.9-13, 27, 33, 45, 53, 59, 69, 81, 85, 113, 137, 147, 167, 191): Marie-Catherine de la Roche
Recipe rewriting: Sophie Brissaud

Translation from French: Wendy Sweetser
Proofreading: Nicole Foster and Tina Isaac-Goizé

Abrams books are available at special discounts when purchased in quantity for premiums and promotions as well as fundraising or educational use. Special editions can also be created to specification. For details, contact specialsales@abramsbooks.com or the address below.

Photoengraving: IGS-CP

Printed and bound in December 2020 by DZS GRAFIK DOO
ISBN: 978-1-4197-4430-3

Legal déposit: October 2019
Printed in Slovenia

ABRAMS
The Art of Books

195 Broadway
New York, NY 10007
abramsbooks.com